THE CAPITOL HILL PLAYBOOK

A Machiavellian Guide for Young Political Professionals

By Nicholas Balthazar

Skyhorse Publishing

Skyhorse Publishing books may be purchased in bulk at special discounts for sales promotion, corporate gifts, fund-raising, or educational purposes. Special editions can also be created to specifications. For details, contact the Special Sales Department, Skyhorse Publishing, 307 West 36th Street, 11th Floor, New York, NY 10018 or info@skyhorsepublishing.com.

Skyhorse® and Skyhorse Publishing® are registered trademarks of Skyhorse Publishing, Inc.®, a Delaware corporation.

Visit our website at www.skyhorsepublishing.com.

10 9 8 7 6 5 4 3 2 1

Library of Congress Cataloging-in-Publication Data is available on file.
ISBN: 978-1-62087-739-5

Printed in the United States of America

Dedicated to my Sweet Sweet and all my brothers-in-arms

How one lives is so far distant from how one ought to live, that he who neglects what is done for what ought to be done, sooner effects his ruin than his preservation.
Niccolò Machiavelli

As the bee in the green meadows is ever wont to rob the flowers among the grass, so our Courtier must steal this grace from all who seem to possess it, taking from each that part which shall most be worthy of praise.
Baldassare Castiglione

TABLE OF CONTENTS

INTRODUCTION

Observe different men of the same calling, and governing
yourself with that good judgment which must ever be your
guide, go about selecting now this thing from one and that
thing from another.

—Castiglione

The first time I felt embarrassed to brag to a stranger that I was an advisor to a prominent politician, I was sitting next to a beautiful young woman who was on her way to London to begin an MBA program at Oxford. We were the same age, but while she was flying to London to attend lectures, I was going to give one. I had been invited by the British government to share my views on upcoming climate change legislation. As I listened to myself describe a schedule that included lunch with the Majority Whip and a meeting at 10 Downing Street with the prime minister's chief climate change advisor, I suddenly felt deeply embarrassed. Had I become "that guy"? The guy who uses his fancy job to pick up women?

She was impressed. She said something about how young I looked and asked how I came to be so successful at such a young age. My cheeks were still too hot at that point for me to face her directly, so I mumbled something about being read a chapter of Machiavelli's *The Prince* before bed each night as a child. I was too embarrassed to say much more after that. I pretended to read a book silently for the rest of the flight. After exchanging brief nods and tight smiles in the passport line at Heathrow, my beautiful seat companion and I parted ways forever.

While success at a young age is noteworthy in most fields, it's not in politics. The nature and demands of political life make it one of the few professions where the young—for the most part—rule. Even if you are fresh out of college, if you are willing to make the sacrifices and pay your dues, there's almost no limit to how fast you can rise. The tricky part is making the right decisions at the right times along the way.

When you're young those decisions can be hard to make. That's where advice from mentors or more experienced people helps. But what if you don't have a network of mentors and experienced friends sitting by the phone waiting for your call?

I obviously can't see you, but I assume you picked up this book because you are interested in entering the political arena and want to understand how to be successful. With this book, you are headed in the right direction.

I was just like you once. I was thinking about pursuing a life in politics, but I didn't have a lot of resources or people I could draw on for advice. This book is written with you specifically in mind. Regardless of whether you have a deep stable of friends to call on or if you are alone like I was, this book will provide you with key information about what you need to rise and survive as a staffer in politics.

But before we go any further, the first thing you need to do is buy, borrow, or steal copies of *The Prince* and the *Book of the Courtier*. The second thing you need to do is to find a comfortable place to sit and read them. If you really want to hit the ground running on your first day as a staffer, it is essential that you read these books.

For centuries, these two books have stood as timeless references for understanding political power. Chances are you are aware of the books, but chances also are that you have not read them. Everyone knows *The Prince*, but very few people have read it. And many of those who have missed the main points of the book. Here is your chance— if you really want to hit the ground running—to apply the key points of these highly useful and influential books.

On the cab ride to the hotel after my encounter with the beautiful woman, I tried to remember what influenced my decision to become a political staffer. I was sort of telling the truth when I said I had been influenced by *The Prince*. After graduation, when I began considering the idea of working for an elected official, my roommate's father, a state senator, suggested I read it. I was not impressed by the book. I found it hard to get through, and to be honest, I couldn't see what the big deal was. Mostly I thought to myself, "This thing was written five hundred years ago; how could it possibly be that relevant today?"

If you've read it, you know one of the main themes of *The Prince* is how to win and maintain a kingdom. At the time I could see at least how the book might be helpful to someone in the modern age who was interested in running for office, but when I first read the book, I wanted to work for an elected official, not be one. I tucked it away on a shelf next to my copy of *The Goblet of Fire* and proceeded to forget about it.

Another friend recommended I read *The Book of the Courtier* by Baldassare Castiglione. It was also about how to succeed in politics, but Castiglione had written the book with the servant in mind, not the politician. Unlike *The Prince*, which was specifically written with the purpose of advising a political figure, or "prince," on how to be successful in politics, *The Courtier* was written for the person who wants to succeed while working for the prince. I was vaguely familiar with the book. It was required reading for an Italian Renaissance course I took in college. But at the time, I hadn't been able to fully appreciate what the book offered.

My friend pointed out that the book was very popular in its day for many of the same reasons *The Prince* became popular: it offered a blueprint for how to conduct oneself in the rough and tumble world of politics. So I gave it a try. But it was even worse! I was struck immediately by the fact that it was written during a time when staffers were judged by totally different standards than they are today, like how well they danced or rode a horse. As I skimmed through the chapters, I thought, "Why are people recommending these lame books to me?" Surely there was something from my own century that I could read. Why did I have to go back five hundred years for a decent guide for young people interested in pursuing a career in politics? It was a couple of years later, after I got a job working for a politician, that I began to fully understand the importance of these books. Now, when I look back, I can't imagine how I let the significance of such valuable resources slip by me. Not only are these books still relevant for the political minded, the messages they convey are eternal and universal and can be applied across professions where interpersonal relationships are key—not just in politics. Today *The Book of the Courtier* and *The Prince* sit on the same shelf where I keep my dictionary and address book.

Not only do *The Prince* and *The Courtier* provide valuable insights into the lives and motivations of political people, they also contain a central and priceless message that would benefit anyone in politics: bad luck doesn't have to ruin you. Everyone gets a little bad luck in their careers; these books show you how to minimize its effects.

All the answers are there. The hard part for someone living in the twenty-first century is figuring out how to separate the relevant from the irrelevant stuff. But if you are as politically naive and inexperienced as I was when I first read them, you may not recognize the full value of their lessons. My job with this book is to be your guide and to direct you to the truly useful parts of those books in order to help you fully appreciate what they have to teach you.

It occurred to me only by chance one day that *The Prince* and *The Courtier* each approach the subject of political survival from opposite perspectives. Machiavelli's strategy for success rests on the theory that everyone in politics is ultimately selfish, and anyone who wants to survive and prosper in that world must act the same way. Machiavelli wants the reader to lift the veil from his eyes and to accept that men often let their inner demons influence their actions. Castiglione lived and prospered in the same world and at about the same time, but he chose to approach the subject from a less selfish standpoint. Instead of encouraging the reader to look out only for his own welfare, the Castiglione model insists that by devoting yourself to service and self-improvement, you will ensure your success in politics.

The Machiavelli strategy can be summarized as one that is based on a realistic view of the world, while Castiglione's is idealistic and aspirational. Machiavelli was trying to encourage his reader to conduct himself in a way that embraced the world for what it was at that time—dangerous and unpredictable. Contrastingly, Castiglione knew that his reader must also live in that world, but he wanted his reader to live as if the world and everything in it aspired to perfection. Any experienced staffer today will tell you that if you follow the Machiavellian strategy too closely you may become powerful, but everyone will hate you. Conversely, if you follow Castiglione too closely, you will have tons of friends but you leave yourself open to being exploited by the Machiavellian types—who, since they don't have any friends—have plenty of time to think of ways to screw you. The only reasonable path for the modern-day courtier lies in between.

The Courtier and *The Prince* were written during the Renaissance, when politics was a deadly blood sport. You needed to keep your head, if you wanted to keep your head. So staffers had to be alert, a little paranoid, and self-centered. Machiavelli's portrait of the prince and courtier fully supports this image. Castiglione, on the other hand, was writing about a world that was beginning to take shape but didn't fully exist at the time—a world where staffers educated and improved themselves solely for the purpose of becoming better advisors.[1]

Before the Renaissance, anyone with stones big enough to seize the crown could become king. The kings tended to be commanding figures who knew what they wanted and didn't really need the advice of the people who worked for them. So, the staffer really didn't matter. Staffers lived only to execute the wishes of the king. But Castiglione was writing about a new world that was emerging, where the rules for royal succession were changing and where, increasingly, only those in direct line to the crown could be king. Idiots and even children were beginning to inherit empires.

Castiglione envisioned a time where staffers could be as influential as the prince. His vision was prophetic. Around the same time that he wrote *The Courtier*, powerful advisors like Cardinal Wolsey and Thomas Cromwell, both of whom helped run England for Henry VIII, were taking the stage, and these glorified staffers did indeed become as powerful as the king they served.

When Baldassare Castiglione died in 1529, he was listed among the greatest courtiers of his day, if not the greatest who ever lived. The Holy Roman Emperor Charles V, upon hearing of his death, called Castiglione the finest gentleman there ever was.

Castiglione possessed many of the qualities and skills he lauded in his book as those possessed by the ideal courtier. He was a warrior and a poet, a scholar and a diplomat. When he died, he was serving out his final post as Papal Nuncio of Spain, a position awarded to him by Pope Clement VII in recognition of his charm and devotion to duty.

It took Castiglione eight years to write *The Book of the Courtier*. Even after finishing the draft in 1516, the famously fastidious Castiglione continued to edit and improve the manuscript until it was finally pried from his clinched fists more than a decade later and published a year before his death.

The book is hardly perfect. Even his contemporary readers must have recognized instantly that the book is not much more than a series of blatant plagiarisms held together with one or two original ideas. But those one or two ideas were strong enough to secure Castiglione's place in history. While painting a remarkably accurate portrait of what it was like to live at a Renaissance court, the book also introduced the world to the concept of "sprezzatura," or the art of doing things with grace and ease, and unpacks in a memorable and instructive way the concept of pursuing the goal of self-improvement for the purpose of being a better servant.

Niccolò Machiavelli was born in Florence at the height of the Renaissance in 1469, the second son of a fallen noble family. He died fifty-eight years later, uncelebrated and obscure. A jaundiced eye might have regarded his life as a failure were it not for his writing of *The Prince*, a book viewed by many as one of the most important books ever written.

Machiavelli toiled away much of his adult life in a series of mid-level government posts until the renowned Medici family wrestled control of the principality away from Machiavelli's patron and he was dismissed from service. He never again held a government post of any significance. He retired to a modest life and focused on writing, but at no point did his career ever attain the level of greatness that writing *The Prince* suggests he was capable of achieving.

Machiavelli died before *The Prince* was published. During his life, he never saw or enjoyed any acclaim for the book, though he would be remembered for centuries afterwards because of it. His death inspired no memorable words of praise from any of the powerful men he served, and to this day no one can say with certainty where his body is buried. Though he died relatively unsung, Machiavelli left behind a body of work that has helped shape the modern world of politics and leadership and continues to illuminate the idea of what it means to be a prince.

The Book of the Courtier and *The Prince* are memorable and valuable for their depictions of life five centuries ago, but they are eternal for what they say about how we should live our lives today.

So what are the key guidelines to bear in mind as you progress through this book? Remember, if you want to be successful and survive in politics in the United States today, you need to be a convincing liar, a quick study, possess good political instincts, and be able to take a punch. It helps also to *seem* to be a nice person—regardless of whether you are or not. My experience is that most of these qualities and skills can be taught. And with the help of Machiavelli and Castiglione, that is what I plan to do.

The Capitol Hill Playbook is divided into two parts. Part one explores the personality and motivations of an elected official or "prince." I discuss how to choose which prince to work for and how to manage your relationship with him or her.

Staffers or "courtiers" are discussed in part two. I describe the ups and downs of being a courtier; the qualities that all good courtiers must possess or not possess; how to win an office battle; and how to choose political friends. Taken altogether, the book provides key elements that make up a realistic portrait of life as a staffer today—warts and all.

As in *The Prince* and in *The Book of the Courtier*, the lessons and advice I give are drawn from the lives of well-known historical figures. I go back as far as Renaissance

Europe and come forward as recently as the Obama administration. My focus is on how to become a successful American staffer, so the vast majority of historical figures will be Americans like Madeline Albright and Colin Powell. But as you read through the book, what will become clear is that regardless of the century, all successful staffers possess basically the same skills and qualities.

Like *The Prince*, this book is written in a voice that is intentionally definitive, authoritative, and conversational. This is not a traditional textbook. I'm sure you have no interest in reading one, and I have no interest in writing one.

Each chapter begins with a vignette dramatization of a scene featuring a famous historical figure that illustrates the main message of the chapter. The vignette is italicized in order to separate it from the rest of the book and to emphasize that, though based in fact, it is nonetheless a dramatization. In some cases, facts and names have been altered in order to protect the identities of the people involved—some of whom are still walking the halls of power. These italicized vignettes are the only time in the book that facts are handled in this way. In all other places, the facts are lifted directly from the historical record. Each vignette is preceded and followed by a quote from either Machiavelli or Castiglione on the subject of the chapter. The ideas presented in the quotes will be analyzed throughout the chapter to assess how each man might have interpreted the chapter's subject. My own interpretations of the subject based on my own experience are also threaded throughout.

Not all of the ideas expressed in this book are positive and some may attract controversy—but they are all based on research or on what I have witnessed with my own eyes. I hope you find *The Capitol Hill Playbook* as informative to read as it was to write.

PART ONE

THE AMERICAN
PRINCE

1 | ON THE FOUR TYPES OF PRINCES

Because men are bad, and will not keep faith with you, you too are not bound to observe it with them.

—Machiavelli

Politicians Are Not Like Us

If American dictionaries in the 1970s had a photo next to the definition of corrupt politician, chances are the picture would have been of Richard M. Nixon, the thirty-seventh president of the United States. Nixon was involved in one of the most embarrassing and damaging scandals in US political history. His role in the plot to break into the headquarters of the Democratic National Committee at the Watergate Hotel led to his being the first American president to resign from office.

On the afternoon of August 9th in 1974, Nixon must have felt like an observer on his own life as he stepped up onto the small stage that had been constructed in the East Room of the White House, flanked by the first lady, Patricia, his two daughters, and their husbands. He might have noticed that Pat Nixon's expressionless eyes conveyed no sign of the weight of the occasion until they met the tear-filled eyes of her youngest daughter, Tricia, standing next to her. The president and his family had arrived to address a gathering of White House aides and staff. The room was silent except for the sound of someone crying softly.

As the president started to speak, his eyes welled up and he began to sweat. He cleared his throat and over the next twenty minutes, haltingly and sometimes ramblingly, delivered what would become one of his last speeches as President of the United States. Just the day before, Richard Nixon, a man who had recently won reelection by one of the largest electoral margins in American history, who had triumphantly brought to an end the stubborn and deeply unpopular Vietnam War, and who had achieved the extraordinary by becoming the first American president to visit Communist China, became the first president to resign.

At the end of his speech, he left the audience with advice that must have been confusing at the time, but in retrospect might have helped to explain to some of those gathered the reason for his downfall: "Those who hate you don't win unless you hate them—and then, you destroy yourself."

Nixon's handling of the Watergate scandal revealed a president that few Americans of the day recognized. Reports from congressional hearings and the release of tapes recorded in the Oval Office showed Nixon to be a paranoid, bitter, and deeply corrupted man willing to hurt anyone and destroy any career to conceal his role in the illegal cover-up. It is reported that when the White House Counsel informed him that a key participant in the Watergate scandal was threatening to discuss Nixon's role with the press if the president did not agree to pay a bribe (that could be as high as $1 million dollars), Nixon replied: "I know where I can find a million dollars!" Nixon left office disgraced and hated by millions of Americans. His administration forever changed Americans' perception of the presidency and of the people who run for office.

"Because Men Are Bad and Will Not Keep Faith with You, You too Are Not Bound to Observe It with Them."

As a person who has worked in politics for almost twenty years, when I think about this story, I can't help but think about those people who worked for Nixon watching as he imploded before their eyes. Of course those who worked closely with him knew what he was really like, but those farther down the food chain must have been deeply disappointed. Anyone who has worked in politics as long as

I have isn't surprised by Nixon's story. At this point in my career, I have reached the conclusion that the world of politics is filled with deeply flawed politicians.

In *The Prince*, much is said about the characteristics of princes, but little is said about their personalities. If Machiavelli were writing his book today, when modern-day princes win their kingdoms in the polling booth instead of on the battlefield, he would undoubtedly have had to delve into the question of why people even want to be princes in the first place. Machiavelli might look at Nixon and speculate about the source of his corruption and he might wonder if Nixon's harsh judgment of himself and his feelings of alienation fueled his political drive.

Machiavelli might have told the story of how Nixon's father was a failed lemon farmer and how his mother was briefly ostracized by her own family for marrying beneath her station. He might have showed how, as a child, Nixon was described as not being the kind of kid you hugged, how he had few friends, and how even his closest friends confessed that they did not really know him.

He might have shown how Nixon's father was a hard-driving disciplinarian and his mother cold and detached and how all these factors combined to make Nixon deeply self-conscious, awkward, and insecure. How, even after decades in politics, human contact on the campaign trail would make Nixon sweat; how he remained awkward in front of audiences; and even as president, how he avoided eye contact and disliked shaking hands.[2]

Machiavelli might have painted this painfully revealing portrait of Richard Nixon in order to show his reader what politicians can be like. But in painting this portrait of the modern politician, Machiavelli would also be showing why it can be such a challenge to work for some of them. Since I'm writing a book that concerns them, I have no choice but to do the same.

I began this chapter with a story about Richard Nixon not only to remind readers, some of whom know little about the man or what a corrupt and damaged politician looks like, but also to introduce a question that is fundamental to understanding success in politics—why do people run for office? As you progress through this book you will see how the answer to that question influences a politician's relationship to everything and everyone around him—including his staff.

It can impact the policies he promotes, the decisions he makes, and even the kind of people he surrounds himself with. To a degree, the authentic answer to that question says more about who he is than any policy or program he promotes. Many politicians run purely for personal gain. If possible, they are the ones you should avoid, though they oftentimes are the ones who are the most successful.

I remember the day I first realized that the people who run for office were more flawed than others. I had joined the reelection campaign of my state's governor after a friend, who had grown tired of listening to me tell him how much I wanted to be a congressman, challenged me to do something about it. What I learned on that campaign, and in the two years that followed, squashed forever any desire I might have had of becoming a politician.

First, let me say that despite what you might see on the Sunday morning talk shows, most politicians are not movers and shakers. The majority of the country's politicians are low-level officials who serve on councils or as small town mayors and who often have other jobs. They take time away from their families and careers to devote themselves to the task of ensuring that your town's sewage system operates properly and that a traffic light is where it needs to be. They sit on school boards and zoning boards and work for very little money—in some cases no money—for the privilege of playing a role in helping to make their communities better.

In the really early days of my career, I naively thought that all politicians chose their occupation out of an altruistic desire to serve the public. But, after working closely with a few, I discovered that wasn't entirely true. In fact, in some cases, it wasn't true at all. The more politicians and aspiring politicians I met and worked with, the more I encountered people who were too selfish to be motivated purely by a desire to serve anyone but themselves. Narcissism was such a common trait among them that I began to wonder why.

I learned the hard way that the people who choose to run for office fit into one of four basic categories: they are damaged, desperate, disenfranchised, or duty-bound. In private, I refer to them as "The Four Ds." What many of them share is a need for external validation so intense that it pushes them to do things that you and I wouldn't.

When you get to know them, what you discover is, they don't just want power and the chance to serve others. What they want more than anything else is to be adored.

On one level, who can blame them? It feels good to be a politician. People lower their voices when you speak. They stand up when you enter a room. Strangers want to shake your hand and seek out your advice. Children tell their parents they want to grow up to be just like you. In short, you are adored. But all this adulation comes at a steep price. That price is the reason that many politicians are not like you and me and why only the really neediest of people, or conversely the most honorable, make politics their chosen profession.

OK, now you're probably thinking, "Why is the life of being a politician so tough?" Well, for one thing, the work is grueling. Early in my career, even from my modest vantage point among the party cannon fodder, I could see how demanding and taxing the daily lives of elected officials were. Spending a day following them around can easily discourage any sane person from running for office.

For many politicians, the day begins early, because there's always a breakfast fund-raiser to attend somewhere. Of course, they don't actually get to eat at the fund-raiser because they're often the featured speaker. But if they're lucky, someone on their staff will grab a bagel and coffee for them to eat on the ride to the office afterwards.

Then, as we mere mortals are trying to build up the courage to get out of bed, they are already at the office and have begun a string of back-to-back meetings that will last most of the morning. After meetings, there's barely enough time to grab another cup of coffee, and maybe hit the bathroom, before heading off to a committee hearing. Sometime between meetings and hearings, they find time to quickly force down a sandwich for lunch, after which, the meetings start up all over again. Then, around dinner time, they'll leave the office for a string of fund-raisers or some other such political event before finally arriving home in time to tuck in the kids. They might get a break from this routine on weekends, but even that's rare. During campaign season, the days start even earlier and last even longer—and there are no weekends off. And, let's say they are successful enough to have accumulated a little power over the years—the life doesn't get any easier.

American politics is perhaps the only profession where the higher you rise and the more power you accumulate, the harder you work. Think about it: lawyers, doctors, teachers—when they reach the senior ranks of their professions, they work less. They can sit back and delegate. In politics, it's the opposite. If you are lucky enough to become speaker of the House or a Senate committee chairman, your days are longer than the days of the people serving below you. This is because you must not only satisfy the daily commitments of your leadership position, you still have to attend to all the other responsibilities related to being an elected official. This means attending cheesy community events and supermarket openings and all the other quaint, but necessary, activities that elected officials suffer through to stay visible and relevant in the eyes of their constituents.

If these weren't enough reasons to drive a sane person into another profession, there's always the ever present threat of job loss hanging over your head to help focus your mind. A good politician is always looking over his shoulder watching out for challengers. Even those politicians who have achieved great power and influence know that their power will not fully protect them from a younger, and even more desperate or damaged, person seeking to unseat them.

In addition, unlike other professions, in politics, when you lose your job, you can't just move to another town or state and run again—you'll be labeled a carpetbagger. The local party system in the new town will surround you and attack you like white blood cells attack a virus. Every politician knows that if he loses a race, it could be the end of his career. That means no more people telling him how great he is and complimenting him on the weight he's lost, no more free trips to Hawaii to play golf, and nothing to do on a Friday night. The phone just stops ringing. And forget about the pay—which, compared to the amount of work necessary to stay in office, is a daily insult.

In spite of all of this, politicians still think the adulation they receive is worth all the hardship because in many cases the adulation satisfies some deep longing they have within themselves that can only be fulfilled by having people constantly telling them how great they are. After struggling to understand why people would subject themselves to the demands of this kind of life, I came up with the idea of the Four Ds.

The Four Ds

Those driven by damage are motivated to run for office because they were the objects of abuse, neglect, or abandonment as children. Daddy left or mommy left or mommy drank or daddy drank or both mommy and daddy drank before leaving. They were beaten or abandoned or ignored. Whatever happened to them as children left them with a desperate need for love and approval so strong that they would do whatever it took to satisfy it. Politics is the perfect profession for these kinds of people because people who do not know them eagerly stroke their egos and give them love for free.

When I search for a historical example of a familiar politician that fits into this category, I immediately think of President Ronald Reagan, whose well-publicized habit of tuning out during arguments was a defense mechanism developed to cope with his alcoholic father. Or Speaker Newt Gingrich who, by his own admission, grew up lonely after his father abandoned him rather than pay child support. He was adopted by his mother's new husband, but their relationship was strained and distant. Or President Bill Clinton whose real father died in a car crash three months before Clinton was born and whose stepfather was abusive and paid little attention to him.

Those driven by desperation are people who are searching for deliverance from mediocrity. These people live unexceptional lives, accomplishing unexceptional things and, one day, they look up just long enough to recognize that they have more days behind them than ahead. They start looking for ways to add meaning to their insignificant lives. They know that if they can raise the relatively small sum necessary to fund a minor campaign, and if they can stick with the campaign long enough to get elected, they get to live out the rest of their days with "Honorable" in front of their names.

When I think of this category of person, as much as I respect him, I think of Harry Truman. President Truman is the Ringo Starr of American presidential politics. He lived much of his life unremarkably. It was only after being given the once-in-a-lifetime chance, at the age of fifty, to run for the US Senate, that he was able to transform his life.

Those driven by disenfranchisement tend to be outsiders. They are motivated to choose a life of public service because they have grown tired of living on the margins of society. These people are often members of an ethnic minority group, they are gay, or they are women. Barack Obama's ethnicity places him squarely in this category, but disgraced President Richard Nixon fits too. Nixon always saw himself as an outsider. He held onto this opinion even after he had achieved what most people would agree was the extraordinary by becoming a congressman, senator, and vice president of the United States. The perception that others viewed him as an outsider fueled his political drive throughout his career. He held on to this belief even in the dying days of his presidency. He even thought that his outsider status, not his breathtaking immorality, was the source for his ultimate downfall.

Those driven by duty are the children of public servants who, from an early age, are encouraged to pursue a life of service. Many times they are the sons and daughters of teachers, letter carriers, diplomats, law enforcement officers, government employees, or, in some cases, even elected officials. Lyndon Baines Johnson, the thirty-sixth president of the United States, was the son of Sam Johnson, a five-term member of the Texas House of Representatives; US Senator Carol Moseley Braun was the daughter of a police officer and a medical technician; and US Senator John McCain was the son of the one-time commander of US naval forces in the Pacific. But even in the case of the duty-bound, there is some invisible hand at work that draws them to politics as opposed to some other mode of service, like nursing or teaching or the law. That hidden hand guides them through the strains and pressures associated with the social demands and public scrutiny of politics and is what separates them from other service-minded people. To most people the pressures of politics are so intense that they are not worth the effort. But to the duty-bound, who are oftentimes touched by one or some combination of the Four Ds, politics is the only truly satisfying profession.

If you choose to pursue a career as a political staffer, you will undoubtedly encounter one of these types of people and will need to understand the source of their motivation. In many ways, this is the most important thing about them.

The story of the Four Ds is a cautionary tale. This is information that you should reflect on if you want to be a part of the world of politics. I've been lucky, but you may not be. Odds are that some of the bosses you work for will turn out to have destructive dynamics driving them. But as I said above, that's not necessarily a bad thing. Working for a damaged prince, as for a boss in any other profession, has its pros and cons. What you need to do is ask yourself what you want most out of your career. Are you willing to work for anyone—*anyone*—to get where you want to go? Are you the type of person who wants to look up to your boss or are you willing to overlook the flaws to focus on the work, regardless of who the boss is? If you are going into politics expecting to find infallible people, you will be disappointed.

To succeed and survive in politics, you need to understand what you are dealing with and you need to remember to look out for yourself. Reflect on what you've read here and take a moment before beginning your career to figure out what you want and what you are willing to endure to achieve it.

2 | ON WORKING FOR A PRINCE

With all the thoughts and forces of your mind, love and almost adore the prince whom you serve, above every other thing, and mould your wishes, habits and all your ways to your prince's liking.

—Castiglione

A Staffer's Burden

Napoleon Bonaparte was about to explode. The only thing that kept him from physically striking Charles Maurice de Talleyrand, his foreign minister, was the thought of having to deal with the backlash from Talleyrand's many friends afterwards. On this cold Saturday afternoon in January 1809, Napoleon came closer to striking him than he has ever come before.

He was angry about French rumors that had reached him on the battlefield five hundred miles away in Spain that he was losing the war. He suspected that the rumors had been started by one of his chief ministers, and that Talleyrand was probably to blame. His suspicions would be confirmed on another day—but on this day—Napoleon felt like beating the confession out of him. Driven by a burst of anger, he rode five days straight from Spain to Paris just for the chance to look Talleyrand in the eyes as he accused him of treason.

He struggled to remain calm and began slowly. He asked if the rumors were true that people were plotting to kill him, but before Talleyrand could respond, Napoleon flew into a rage, shaking his fists in his face and calling him a liar and a coward. Napoleon abandoned all pretense of calm and unleashed a wall of invective at his foreign minister. With extraordinary composure, Talleyrand stood face-to-face with Napoleon and absorbed the shrieking insults and ignored the flecks of spit that struck his face as Napoleon leaned ever closer in his fury. Neither the feeling of Napoleon's hot breath on his cheek nor the scent of decaying meat on his breath broke Talleyrand's impenetrable facade.

Napoleon screamed that Talleyrand would sell out his father if he could and that he should break him like a piece of glass under his boot for his deceitfulness. Then, as he turned to leave the room, before crossing the threshold, he hurled one last insult in Talleyrand's direction: "You are a shit in a silk stocking!" With those words, he stormed out of the room.

As his fellow courtiers watched in stunned silence, Talleyrand calmly gathered his coat and his hat and gloves. The room that rang with the violent shouts of Napoleon only moments before was now silent except for the sound of the wooden floor boards creaking under Talleyrand's shifting weight as he adjusted the scarf around his neck in the mirror. Satisfied with his knot, he turned, and with a blank expression quietly and slowly walked past his colleagues out of the room in search of the emperor.

"A Courtier Must Devote All His Thought and Strength to Loving and Almost Adoring the Prince."

Talleyrand disliked Napoleon, but Napoleon despised Talleyrand.[3] Why? I could say that Napoleon was an unbelievably insecure person and that he was the very definition of a disenfranchised prince. He saw himself as an outsider because, in a society that valued old family names and pure bloodlines, Napoleon was reminded daily of his low birth to foreign parents on an island off the coast of the French mainland. In the beginning, his admiration for Talleyrand's pedigree was the basis of their friendship. In the end, it fueled Napoleon's resentment. Despite these reasons, it was not Napoleon's jealousy of Talleyrand's bloodlines that would eventually make them enemies; the wedge that drove them apart was the fact that Talleyrand refused to remain devoted to Napoleon.

Napoleon and Talleyrand began their relationship as close friends. As Napoleon rose to power, Talleyrand recognized immediately his potential for greatness and devoted himself to becoming Napoleon's most trusted aide. He spent long hours discussing matters of state with the emperor, and along the way they developed a strong personal bond based on trust and mutual admiration. This all changed when Napoleon's military exploits grew increasingly destructive to France and the French people. Talleyrand's devotion to Napoleon diminished with each new military campaign, and eventually Talleyrand began actively working behind the scenes to undermine the emperor.

Castiglione advises his readers that if a courtier wants to be successful, he must be completely devoted to his prince. To a point, Castiglione's advice is correct. For a staffer, the quickest path to the heart of any prince is to show him that you are devoted to him by working long hours, accepting any burden without complaint, and executing any request without hesitation. The problem is that Castiglione's advice is incomplete. For the reasons I've mentioned in the previous chapter and will explore in more detail in later chapters, a staffer should not put anyone else's interests above his or her own self preservation. If a staffer blindly puts their fate totally in the hands of others, he or she sows the seeds of his or her own destruction. Talleyrand began to recognize that by blindly devoting himself to helping Napoleon achieve his imperial aspirations, he was hurting himself and destroying France. Slowly, Talleyrand's devotion to Napoleon gave way to a kind of *qualified devotion*. If you want to survive in politics, it is precisely this type of devotion that I am recommending you pursue in your relationship with the prince.

When Castiglione wrote *The Book of the Courtier*, his ambition was to capture on paper the skills and qualities that made for the ideal courtier. He wanted the book to be a guide that the reader could refer to and chart a successful life at court.

The book is written in a series of dialogues between courtiers partially for entertainment value and partially to facilitate a critical exchange on the ideas laid out for the reader. The book is valued today in the academic community for its vivid and realistic depiction of life at that time. But political historians also value the book for its illustrations of the political and interpersonal dynamics and mores of the day. Castiglione tries to capture and present the essence of court life by focusing on those key elements that help to ensure a courtier's success. He wants the reader to understand that showing devotion to one's prince is an essential element of that success.

In the quote leading this section, Castiglione advises the reader that he must be devoted to his prince, but Castiglione does not unpack in great detail the pros and cons of devotion. I think he wanted to avoid showing the seedier side of life as a courtier that blind devotion can precipitate. He wanted to show what was necessary about being a courtier, even though he must have known that no one can be absolutely and totally devoted to his or her boss. Think about it. On its face, blind devotion is ridiculous. Is helping your boss really more important than helping your mother? Of course it's not. He gives himself a little bit of an exit though when he suggests that a courtier should leave his prince if he discovers that the prince is immoral. But what if he's not immoral? The question remains: Should any staffer really be completely and totally devoted to his boss? Well, let's take a minute and look at some of the benefits.

In addition to Talleyrand, let's consider the cases of Colonel Edward House, who was a close companion of President Woodrow Wilson, and Harry Hopkins, who was an advisor to President Franklin Roosevelt. Hopkins, House, and Talleyrand[4], each by virtue of his unquestioned devotion to his boss, were able to become extraordinarily powerful staffers, but each paid a price for that power.

The Price Of Devotion

The dynamics of driven people who run for public office drive their need for staffers who are committed completely to them or their cause. During Napoleon's time, a staffer had to swear his allegiance to his sovereign; today, in the United States, you don't have to do that—but that doesn't mean that your boss doesn't secretly want you to. Being a courtier today is very difficult work—maybe even more so than in

Napoleon's time. Today's courtier has to serve not only the prince but the people too. The modern-day prince wants to know that you will do anything to help him personally and that you will do anything to help his constituents—which by extension also helps him. If a prince recognizes this quality in you, the rewards can be endless—but so can the costs.

"Hopkins Would Jump Off A Bridge If Roosevelt Asked Him."

To say that Harry Hopkins was totally devoted to Franklin Delano Roosevelt (FDR) would be a gross understatement. Hopkins devoted himself to Roosevelt completely to the detriment of his relationships and his health.

Hopkins first came to Roosevelt's attention as an extraordinarily capable social worker from Iowa state government. He joined Roosevelt's staff while he was governor of New York, but when he became president, Roosevelt asked House to help him shape and flesh out the details of the New Deal social programs. Over the years, Hopkins would eventually grow to become so powerful that he alone among the president's staff had the authority to overturn a direct presidential order and he alone could speak for the government of the United States without first conferring with the president. Roosevelt trusted Hopkins completely.

Hopkins's areas of influence grew beyond domestic issues to eventually include international affairs—where he became one of Roosevelt's chief diplomatic negotiators and he was often allowed to negotiate directly on Roosevelt's behalf with Winston Churchill, the British prime minister. In fact, during World War II, Hopkins eventually became the top American official responsible for dealing with the Soviet Union.

Hopkins achieved this extraordinary status by doing two things: first, he devoted himself to understanding the president, and second, he devoted himself to divining whatever it was the president wanted and then doing whatever it took to achieve that objective. By this approach, he developed such a keen understanding of Roosevelt's mind that if Roosevelt had difficulty explaining something to a staffer, he would send him or her to Hopkins for clarification.

His power and influence over international affairs grew to such a degree that once, on hearing about a cable the president had asked be sent to Winston Churchill in advance of an important strategy meeting between Churchill and Soviet Premier Josef Stalin, Hopkins rushed down to the radio room and ordered that the transmission be stopped, even though it was the president himself who had ordered its transmission. The radio operator followed Hopkins's order immediately without question. After giving the order, Hopkins went up to the president's bedroom to explain. Roosevelt quickly recognized the major mistake that would have been committed if the transmission had gone through. This incident further cemented Roosevelt's appreciation for Hopkins.

FDR cultivated, educated, and tutored Hopkins in politics, grooming him for ever greater responsibility, not just because he liked him, but because he believed Hopkins lived only to serve him.

Colonel House Was Not a Real Colonel

Colonel Edward House's title was ceremonial and given to him the same way it was awarded to any other southern gentlemen in the post–Civil War South who had distinguished himself in some way. Part of the reason the colonel received this honor was for his brilliant abilities as a political strategist. This talent is what first brought him to the attention of presidential candidate Woodrow Wilson. Colonel House helped Wilson win the presidency in 1913, and as they worked closely together afterwards, each man discovered that he felt a special connection to the other. His close bond with the president made House the president's most trusted advisor and, eventually, one of the most powerful men in the world. Wilson explained to others that the reason he trusted House so completely was because House always seemed so selfless.

The world of presidential politics can be draining. Everyone is pulling at the politician asking for one thing or another, making it difficult for him to really relax. Because House seemed to want nothing from Wilson, the president was able to relax around him and they developed a close friendship. Wilson not only trusted House, but more importantly, he felt as if he could be himself around him. Wilson saw House as the only person in his professional life that he believed wanted nothing from him but to serve him.

Because of their bond, and House's excellent political instincts, Wilson involved House in almost every aspect of his decision making. It would be in international affairs that House achieved his greatest success and attained his greatest power and influence. When Wilson participated in the Paris Peace Conference after the end of World War I, he leaned heavily on House for advice and support. Though the US secretary of state and the defense secretary also attended the conference, and though House held no official government portfolio, the task of acting as lead US negotiator during Wilson's absences fell not to either of them, but to House. Even then, the United States was a recognized superpower, and the authority conferred upon House to represent the president was extraordinary for this college dropout, who possessed only a ceremonial military title to recommend him to his distinguished fellow negotiators.

Eventually, his good political instincts and unquestioned devotion to Wilson enabled House to become the president's chief domestic and international policy advisor and one of history's most powerful courtiers.

Talleyrand the Traitor

In the early days of their relationship, Napoleon received a letter from Talleyrand in which he said that his devotion for Napoleon would last until the end of his life. This over-the-top style of flattery was characteristic of nineteenth-century France and Talleyrand was its most generous and frequent user. It worked particularly well on Napoleon, whose insecurity about the low origins of his birth and whose admiration for Talleyrand's ancient bloodlines turned every obsequious word that fell from Talleyrand's lips into a brightly colored present with Napoleon's name on it.

The bond of their friendship was forged while Napoleon was still a general in the service of the Directory, the government that ran post-Revolutionary France. Both Napoleon and Talleyrand were unhappy with the way the leaders of the Directory were running things, and during long private talks in Talleyrand's residence in Paris and in flowery letters exchanged when Napoleon was away on the battlefield, they planned the overthrow of the government.

Talleyrand stood by Napoleon when the day came, and together they executed a flawless, bloodless coup that installed Napoleon as First Consul, the de facto head of France's government. Napoleon quickly appointed Talleyrand as foreign minister and then elevated him above all other cabinet ministers to a post that made him the second most powerful man in the country—after Napoleon.

Talleyrand then went to work doing everything he could to solidify Napoleon's rule. Napoleon's star continued to rise and he would eventually become not only king but emperor. They worked as a team as Napoleon's armies swept across Europe—Napoleon won the battles and Talleyrand wrote the treaties. Talleyrand devoted all of his time and energy to helping Napoleon rise to greater heights of power. For his loyalty and good counsel, Napoleon showered Talleyrand with titles, lands, and riches. And Talleyrand, being the greedy man that he was, accepted Napoleon's gifts with both hands.

After reading these three stories, you are probably thinking—devotion works! Look at House, look at Hopkins, look at Talleyrand. They were devoted and things worked out for them! Well, not quite. In Hopkins's case, he was so devoted he worked himself into an early grave. All the stress of working for Roosevelt eventually wore on him so much that it exacerbated a stomach ailment that he had been struggling with for much of his adult life. It turned into full blown cancer and he died while still on the president's payroll.

House's devotion inspired so much jealousy in Mrs. Wilson that she launched a clandestine campaign to discredit him and eventually succeeded in turning Wilson against him. He was pushed out of the White House and he went back to Texas in disgrace.

Talleyrand grew tired of playing the devoted servant while Napoleon's constant military campaigns slowly drained France of its wealth and its young men. Eventually he had to acknowledge the fact that he was enabling Napoleon's bloodlust. He decided to help to force Napoleon from power, but, to do so, he had to betray his nation.

The drawbacks of devotion don't have to be this intense; they can be subtle. Consider the story of another no-less-devoted staffer, Henry Kissinger.

You'll remember Henry Kissinger was Nixon's national security advisor. He was the immigrant son of Jewish parents who had escaped the Holocaust to come to America. He had an understandable aversion to anti-Semitic speech and conduct, but while working for President Nixon, he willingly endured the president's racist and anti-Semitic ravings. Nixon purposefully used racially offensive language around Kissinger on some occasions, knowing that he wouldn't object. Regardless of how offensive the president was, Kissinger always pretended to ignore it even while inside he must have been cringing. Why did Kissinger endure these obscenities?

Responding to a colleague, he once said he knew that those who opposed the president or who didn't seem like they were team players were pushed to the margins and became irrelevant. He had witnessed this happening to others and did not want the same to happen to him. Kissinger was extraordinarily ambitious and would let nothing stand in his way, even the racist sentiments of his boss. He knew that Nixon would only allow the most devoted staffers inside his inner circle, so he willingly accepted the abuse. How far is too far when it comes to devotion?

Like Nixon, some politicians are driven by damage in their history. A damaged prince knows his reputation, and he knows that you know it. To win the trust of such a person, you must learn to *appear* devoted. I say *appear* because you don't want to be so devoted that you end up harming yourself the way that Hopkins did or lose your self-respect the way that Talleyrand did. So, while you must at all times appear totally devoted to win and hold the respect of damage-driven princes, you must never actually be devoted. This is necessary because if your boss is flawed—which chances are he is—and if he falls—which he may, then you may fall with him.

To survive in politics, you need to protect yourself, but you must do so in a way that never inspires any doubts about your qualified devotion to your boss. A politician, by his nature, is untrusting and will seek ways to test your devotion as a condition of his trust. If you should lose your boss's trust, you will only regain it at the greatest of pains. Appearing devoted is simple, but it requires self-discipline. You will be rewarded if at all times you appear committed to the mission, station, and person of the prince. If the politician is damaged, he will need to know that you are devoted to him above all else; if he is desperate, he will need to know that you are devoted to helping him preserve his status; and if he is disenfranchised, he will need to know that you are devoted to whatever cause he chooses to promote. Find a way to convince the prince that you are devoted to him and you will gain his confidence and he will reward you.

3 | ON CHOOSING A PRINCE

He who relies entirely upon fortune is lost when it changes.

—Machiavelli

The Wake-Up Call

The US Capitol sits on a hill flanked by a lightly wooded park on one side and a trio of massive white marble congressional office buildings on the other. The middle office building, Longworth, constructed in the image of the US Treasury building, was completed in 1933 and named after Nicholas Longworth, the Depression-era speaker of the House who had the distinction of being the last Republican to serve in that post until Newt Gingrich was elected in 1996. Each of its eight floors has walls painted the same shade of eggshell, punctuated at regular intervals by anonymous brown wooden doors. Behind each door lies the suite that houses the office of a member of Congress. On the main door of each suite hangs a plaque bearing the name of the member and the district he or she represents— that is, every door but one.

The name of Christopher Lee, the congressman elected to represent the people of New York's 26th district, was removed on February 14, 2011, when Congressman Lee resigned his office in the face of a sexual scandal. The forty-six-year-old married father resigned after an Internet gossip news channel posted emails and a shirtless photo that he had sent to a woman in response to a Craigslist dating ad.

Congressman Lee abruptly announced that he was quitting Congress because he feared becoming a "distraction." As members of his staff read a puzzlingly cryptic email from him thanking them for their service and announcing that he would be resigning immediately, the clerk of the House of Representatives read his letter of resignation on the House floor.

To all of us Capitol Hill staffers gathered around the water cooler who remembered that only one year prior another married male member of Congress resigned in the wake of a far worse sexual scandal involving inappropriate contact with a number of young male interns and staffers, Congressman Lee's admission seemed almost tame in comparison. Someone mumbled something about his conservative Republican district and the inviolate sanctity of marriage, and we all shrugged our shoulders and nodded in agreement. Someone else joked about how in France,

Congressman Lee's conduct qualified him for higher office. We all laughed and went back to our desks. A week later, the other shoe dropped.

The Huffington Post, the Internet newspaper, reported that it had been contacted by two Washington DC area transgender men who had each exchanged emails with Congressman Lee. One reported that he had reached out to the congressman in response to an ad Lee had posted on Craigslist. The other man forwarded a never-before-seen photo of the congressman that he said he received after they began chatting by email. As the news hit the monitors of our desktops, a collective "aaahhh-hhhaaa" rose up from our cubicles.

"He Who Relies Entirely upon Fortune Is Lost When It Changes."

When a member of Congress resigns, his staff is effectively out of work as well. I can imagine Congressman Lee's staffers coming in to work that morning happily secure in the knowledge that they were all working for a successful and respected member of Congress, only to leave at the end of the day as out-of-work former employees of a sexual deviant who cheated on his wife and disappointed his young son. For the staffers with established careers and good reputations, work would have been relatively easy to find, but I wouldn't be surprised if the young, unestablished staffers had to resort to accepting unpaid internships just to get their feet back in the door.

One of the main themes of *The Prince* is that, to a degree, you can and should endeavor to control your own fate. To illustrate this point, Machiavelli uses an analogy about how a town may be destroyed by flood one year, but if the city fathers get together and design a plan to build canals, levies, and dykes, the next year the city may be protected from a similar fate. Put simply, bad luck happens, but there are things you can do to minimize its effects.

For you, Machiavelli's message would be: don't rely purely on luck to propel your career. In politics, it's easy to get swept up in the whirlwind lifestyle where days are filled with meeting exciting new people, and around every corner is a new challenge to distract you from your main goal. In politics, it can be easy to get seduced by the feeling that everything you do is vitally important and to lose track of time—but you must resist these distractions. You need to always have a plan for where you want to go next and be working to get there.

Think about the staffers who worked for Congressman Lee. When he fell, some of his staff landed on their feet; others did not. The ones who survived had prepared for the eventuality that things might change, so when the bombshell hit, they were better off than most of their colleagues.

If Machiavelli were advising you today, he would say, princes are flawed people; don't make the mistake of letting their flaws ruin you. Keep your eyes open and your wits about you. He would say: when deciding who to work for, you need to be mindful of the effects of that choice on your future. Taking your fate into your own hands means recognizing that in politics choosing someone to work for has consequences that can be potentially good or bad.

I always think of the staffers in situations like Congressman Lee's, because it reminds me of how much of my own success and prosperity depends on the conduct of my boss. In other fields, if you lose your boss for some reason, someone quickly replaces him, and you are relatively unaffected. But in politics, a lost election or scandal can put a staffer on the street, by no fault of his or her own. Even if you are lucky and your first job is on a committee staff, if the chairman loses an election, you lose too. The committee may get a new chairman right away, but when he takes his seat, you better believe one of his own people will be holding the chair. So, as a person interested in a life in politics, if you have a choice about who to work for, you will want to make sure you analyze the options and make the right choice from the beginning.

Eyes Wide Shut

I think both Machiavelli and Castiglione would back me up when I say that a staffer needs to take his career into his own hands while also being flexible if he wants to survive in the fickle world of politics. You shouldn't *blindly* hitch your wagon to anyone else's star. You need to go in with both eyes open.

If you want to have a long and brilliant career as a staffer, choosing who to work for will always be one of your most important decisions. Choosing the right person can bring many benefits and can make life in politics worth all your sacrifices. But the wrong decision can have long-term and perhaps debilitating consequences for your career.

You should know that people will judge you based on who your boss is. If you work for a controversial figure with controversial views, people will assume that you share your boss's views; otherwise, why else would you choose to work for them? Before accepting or seeking out a job with a political figure, examine your own views and make sure that you share the same philosophy and are willing to accept those views as if they were your own.

You are young and only beginning your career, so you might be asking yourself, why should my political philosophy matter? Well, in most other professions, your doubts would be justified; political philosophy is a marginal issue. But in politics, philosophy is everything because you are expected to help your boss sell his positions and initiatives, and he wants to know that you will be truly supportive.

People will make sweeping assumptions about you, and those perceptions will follow you throughout your career. Not only will you find it difficult to work for one party if you have a history of working for another party, who you work for within a party can impact your future as well. Politics, unlike college, is not an arena where experimentation is encouraged. You have to decide what you believe—now. If you decide to intern or work for a Democrat, you can't change your mind later and work for a Republican. Well, you can, but if you get the job, your colleagues will always be a little suspicious of you, and you may have difficulty getting into the inner circle.

Once you've decided that you share, or at least can tolerate, your boss's political philosophy, then you need to look at the man and decide if you accept who he is as a person.

The first question you need to ask is: What's your boss's reputation? Can his or her flaws lead to you being out of work before you even have a chance to get started? This could be a difficult question to answer. Most times, a politician's flaws are well concealed or deliberately hidden by his closest advisors. If you are not careful, you may not know the danger of working for someone until it's too late.

Your first move should be to do some research. Any prospective employee searching for information about Christopher Lee would have eventually stumbled upon the *Buffalo News* article describing how he was fired from his job at Ingram Micro, the technology products company, for hacking into the company computer. According to news reports, he did so in order to raise the credit limits of his clients so he could increase his sales numbers. This might seem like a minor event, but it's not. It shows what kind of man Lee was at the time and helps to shed light on who he is today. Something like this is an absolute red flag, and some of his staffers were probably aware of this transgression before they joined his staff. I'm sure some of his staffers overlooked this just for the chance to get a job on Capitol Hill. But I imagine those staffers regret their decisions now.

Though information about the true character of a prospective boss may be difficult to access, what you shouldn't have difficulty finding out is what the boss is like to work for. This alone can tell you a great deal about the person—and may even give you insight into his drivers, which of the Four Ds might be operating. The best bosses will have reputations for challenging their employees. The worst bosses will have reputations for abusing them. Keep your eyes and ears open for rumors or red flags—like philandering or questionable morals or a shady past. Ask around if there is high turnover in the office—that is a good indicator of possible problems.

There's something about human nature that always makes us eventually expose our demons if we have them. Politicians can never seem to keep their flaws to themselves. Since politicians are more damaged than most of us, it's not just a matter of how the problems in their personal histories will present themselves—it's a matter of when. It's important that you research your potential boss before you take a job with him. But don't get me wrong. I'm not advising you to run when you see or hear evidence of baggage. Maybe it's worth sticking around despite the damage. Maybe what you can get out of the relationship with him is worth dealing with his flaws. Knowledge of how much and the extent of your boss's damage will help you decide whether to join his staff or when to leave. You must enter this relationship with your eyes open.

As I said above, maybe suffering the abuse is worth it. Sometimes, the flaw is the source of their greatness. Maybe growing up without a real father made President Clinton the master politician that he was. Maybe Richard Nixon's twisted insecurities fueled his foreign policy brilliance. Who knows? What is clear is that the most damaged politicians are often the ones with the most to prove and oftentimes the ones most determined to accumulate power. So, if you want to be the kind of staffer who has great influence and power, maybe you should look the other way when you see trouble.

Alexander Haig[5] was an Army officer when he served as a staffer on the National Security Council for President Nixon. His relationship with Nixon and National Security Advisor Henry Kissinger illustrates the rewards of overlooking a leader's flaws for the sake of your career. In the six years that Haig worked in the White House as an assistant to Henry Kissinger, he went from being a colonel, with an impressive, but hardly stellar professional past, to becoming a four-star general and eventually White House chief of staff.

To achieve this, he had to work for and suffer abuse from two of the most extraordinarily damaged people to ever inhabit the White House. It's almost impossible to find more damaged bosses than Henry Kissinger and President Nixon. Kissinger's and Nixon's paranoia and vindictiveness drove away many of the people who worked closely with them. But Haig remained. And not only did he survive, he flourished. Haig's rise was as much about capacity for absorbing abuse as it was about luck and ability. He was an extraordinary staffer with a soldier's bearing and professionalism, with an impressive command of detail, excellent briefing abilities, discretion, and loyalty. But had Haig not worked for Kissinger and Nixon at such a tumultuous time in the nation's history, with the unpopular Vietnam War raging and Watergate on the horizon, when so many more gifted staffers were leaving, he might never have risen as fast or as far as he did.

Working for an elected official is unlike working for any other type of professional. The job of a politician is not only personality driven, it's also personality sustained. It's like a pyramid balanced upside down on its point—with the tip representing the boss and his staff as the wide base hanging over his head. In any other profession, the pyramid is right side up, and if the base crumbles, the person at the top falls. But in politics, the pyramid is inverted. If the boss crumbles, the team he has assembled to support him crumbles with him. As a person interested in joining the world of politics, you must remember to keep your eyes open and your ears sharp. If you do so, maybe you will have time to jump free of the rubble when the pyramid comes crashing down.

4 | ON MANAGING A PRINCE

The Ideal Courtier has the judgment to perceive what his prince likes, and the wit and prudence to bend himself thereto.
—Castiglione

From Courtesan to Courtier

King Louis XV of France was easily bored. Since there could be only one king, and since he was it, his boredom was everyone else's problem—but no one's more so than his mistress's, Madame de Pompadour.

Louis XV was a painfully shy and insecure man who felt burdened by the daily public duties and expectations of being king. These duties fueled his unhappiness and drove him deeper and deeper into a depression that could be held at bay only with stimulation and distraction. This placed a heavy burden on Pompadour. She was an ambitious woman, determined to hold onto the rank she held at court as the king's chief courtesan. Keeping the notoriously fidgety king interested and entertained became her life's work.

In eighteenth-century France, women who craved power could not be courtiers, and therefore, they could not be official advisors to the king, but they could hold a position of comparable rank and power—official mistress. The same energy that ambitious courtiers devoted to learning the ways of war and court politics, she devoted to keeping the king entertained. No, this didn't just mean sex. Even the allure of sex can wear thin over time. And anyway, Louis XV was king—he had options.

To hold his interest as the years passed and her beauty faded, Madame de Pompadour had to make understanding the king her chief occupation, and she understood him well enough to know that what he wanted most was not sex, but a safe, comfortable place where he could be surrounded by friends and where he could escape the daily pressures of being king. For years, she filled his days with the things he loved—plays and concerts and intimate dinners with friends, hunting parties, and unending tours of his kingdom. Pompadour devoted her professional and private life to the task of managing his moods and easing his boredom. In return, the king made her rich and powerful.

Pompadour was born in 1721 in pre-Revolutionary Paris to an ambitious and pragmatic mother who was not above using her considerable beauty to secure the favors of powerful men. Putting her shoulder into her work, Pompadour's mother was able to single-handedly provide her two children with a solid middle-class upbringing. As was the custom of the day, Pompadour studied voice and acting and was taught to ride a horse like a lady. By the time Louis XV first encountered her during a royal reception, she had grown into an intelligent, confident, and glowing beauty with a graceful manner and a talent for music. He found her utterly irresistible. By the time she died, at the age of forty-two, she had risen from common beginnings to the rank of duchess and was one of the most powerful people in France—male or female.

Madame de Pompadour was lucky. She was born in a country where a king's mistress could hold high rank at court almost equivalent to that of the queen. She also happened to become mistress to a king who disliked the duties and formalities of being king and was happy to delegate many of his duties to others. In the end, not only did she assist the king in disseminating favors, she helped him appoint people to high office. She even negotiated treaties with foreign dignitaries on his behalf.

But Pompadour was also a realist. She understood that her place at court depended on how she managed her relationship with the king. She learned to read his moods, and how to manipulate them. She learned when to approach him for favors and how to present bad news. No one at court knew him better. She parlayed her knowledge of the king and her skill at managing him to achieve a level of power and influence so great that not even the queen of France herself would directly challenge her.[6]

"The Courtier Must Have the Discretion to Discern What Pleases His Prince and the Wit and Judgment to Know How to Act Accordingly."

Without luck and beauty, Pompadour would never have had the opportunities she had at court. But it was her dedication to understanding and managing the prince that made her successful. Poor management of your relationship with your boss can be career suicide. But, if done right, it can open a world of opportunities to you.

Castiglione's book is filled with little suggestions about how to manage your relationship with your prince. All of his suggestions center on building an understanding of your boss and then acting in effective ways to capitalize on that knowledge.

Madame de Pompadour understood Louis XV well enough to know that her position at court was the most vulnerable during the wintertime when bad weather kept the king from the thing that gave him the most satisfaction—hunting. In the spring and summer, the king's mind was easily distracted from the pressures of court life, but when snow or the cold kept him from his horse, he grew depressed and would look around for other forms of entertainment. When that entertainment didn't involve Pompadour, she worried.

To amuse him, Pompadour began organizing and starring in elaborate plays and musicals that required a degree of preparation similar to what might be expected of a full-time artistic director of a theater. She oversaw the writing and creation of scripts and music; she oversaw set development and costume design; she interviewed and cast actors; and she performed many of the lead roles herself. And to ensure that the king's interest was held, she was always striving to find new material. She did all of this just to keep the king from getting bored. All aspects of her existence were devoted to his amusement—can you imagine!

Castiglione would not have been surprised by the extent of her dedication. Her actions were in line with his advice. Pompadour's prosperity depended on the mood of the king, and so she devoted herself to understanding and manipulating his moods. Castiglione didn't invent this concept; the most successful courtiers before and since have appreciated the vital importance of this understanding.

Jumping ahead 250 years, think about Michael Deaver, who was a longtime staffer to President Reagan and who became a key member of the Reagan White House because of his extraordinary ability to read and manage the president. He was so good at it that managing Reagan was pretty much all he did. He got an office in the White House and a secretary and access to Air Force One, just because people knew if they needed something from Reagan, they needed to pay a visit to Deaver first. Unlike Pompadour, however, Deaver's job required that he not only understand Reagan well, but also his wife.

Politicians rarely win elections without the support of their spouses. Often they work as a team where the strengths of one are balanced with the weakness of the other. They work together to get elected, and they work together to stay elected. A successful staffer will cultivate a good relationship not only with the elected official but also with the elected official's spouse.

When Deaver joined Reagan's staff during his campaign for governor in the 1960s, he was assigned the unenviable task of responding to the annoyingly frequent requests of Nancy Reagan. Mrs. Reagan was involved in many of the details of her husband's campaign. If that wasn't enough to drive the campaign staff crazy, her demanding, perfection-driven personality and cold directness would, according to those who worked for her at the time, inspire fear in the hearts of anyone on the receiving end of the phrase: "Mrs. Reagan on line one."

Reagan's campaign manager, recognizing Deaver's affable, charming personality, assigned the care and feeding of Nancy Reagan to him. That job would change his life forever. He took the time to really get to know Nancy and came to admire her deeply. The two developed a close political friendship based on mutual professional respect—and political necessity. She helped him understand and advise Reagan, and he helped provide another access point to the inner workings of the administration for her. The Reagans were intensely private people. The friendship Deaver established with them in those early days provided not only entrée into the Reagan's inner circle, it also made Deaver one of the most powerful members of Reagan's staff.

Deaver's success with the Reagans illustrates how developing an understanding of the prince, his strengths and weakness, his likes and dislikes, can help a courtier better serve the prince and help make a courtier indispensable. You may not have the same opportunity to form the kind of bond Deaver formed with Nancy and Ronnie, but there are things you can do, based on your understanding of the prince, that can make you comparably valuable in your prince's eyes.[7]

For example, some politicians who are good public speakers may not be good writers. An attentive courtier will recognize a prince's deficiencies and commit himself to developing the skills necessary to compensate for them. The lesson of the lives of House and Hopkins and Deaver and Pompadour is that if you want to be a successful staffer, managing your boss is a serious and necessary part of the job.

So, how do you manage a prince? Well, the number one key is to build your understanding of him. You don't have to like him, you just need to understand him. Pompadour and Deaver and House and Hopkins knew that the better they understood the prince, the easier it would be to get him to do what they wanted. You have to understand how and when to approach him with requests; you have to understand what he will support and what he will fight against; you have to understand how to present information to him and how to get him to make a decision. To do this, you have to start with who he is and build out from there. Your strategies must be based on him and his needs—not you and yours. Let's look briefly at some of the tools you will need to make that happen.

Power Tools

Assessing His Needs

To effectively manage your boss, you will need to know what his needs are, where his weaknesses lie, and what his strengths are. Everyone has strengths and weaknesses. Maybe your boss is absentminded. Maybe he is a poor public speaker. Maybe he is not a details person. As an ambitious staffer, you should view your boss's weaknesses as opportunities. If he is absentminded, you should aim to become his memory; if he has difficulty managing detail, you should be the opposite. And if he is a poor public speaker, you should strive to be a good writer. The faster you identify his weakness, the quicker you can identify ways to make yourself indispensible to him.

Napoleon Bonaparte was a brilliant military strategist and inspiring leader, but he was also frighteningly insecure, hot-tempered, and dangerously impetuous. Talleyrand was the opposite and he understood Napoleon thoroughly. It was his understanding of Napoleon that helped make him the most important member of Napoleon's staff. He understood the source of Napoleon's insecurities, his strengths, and his weakness. He immediately recognized that Napoleon's phlegmatic and impulsive tendencies could lead to his own destruction and that he would need advisors who counseled caution. Early in his relationship with Napoleon, Talleyrand resolved to always be a voice of moderation to the emperor. He became the sounding board for Napoleon's ideas, his facilitator, and his conscience.

President Franklin Roosevelt was a dreamer and a planner. His assistant, Harry Hopkins, was a problem solver and a "red-tape cutter." Together, they changed the world. Hopkins knew that FDR was a dreamer and sometimes needed help coming back down to earth. While others encouraged this quality in the president, Hopkins recognized how doing so was a distraction for Roosevelt. He would sit in on meetings with FDR and Churchill while they discussed war strategy during World War II. Whenever Roosevelt would take the conversation soaring up into the clouds, Hopkins would be there, sitting by his side, gently directing him back down to earth.

Like Talleyrand and Hopkins, you need to figure out what your strengths are and how they can help to complement the weaknesses of your boss. I promise you that the energy you devote to this task will not be wasted; it will be recognized, and you will be rewarded for it.

Advising a Prince

There are at least three ways for you to provide advice to your boss. You can be a "company-man" and just parrot back what the prince says or wants; you can offer strong, biased positions with recommendations made with extreme prejudice; or you can dispassionately but earnestly present the two sides of an issue and let the prince make the final decision. I wish I could say that there is a best way of the three, but how you advise your boss is totally dependent on what works best for him—it's your job to figure out his preference.

Every leader has a preferred way of being advised. Ronald Reagan was not a details person and avoided policy making. He preferred his advisors to come to him with fully formed ideas and recommendations so that all he had to do was pull the trigger.

In contrast, President George W. Bush ran his White House like a company and treated policy making like building and executing a business plan. He treated his staffers like "company men" and expected them to recognize the direction he wanted to go in and to fall into line without question. His CEO management style discouraged dissent. If you were one of his staffers and wanted to stay on board, you needed to get on board.

Before you begin to give advice to your boss, but after you've figured out what advising style he prefers, you need to sit down and think about what kind of advisor you want to be. Is it more important to you that you give good, balanced advice, regardless of whether it's what the boss wants to hear? Or, do you want to be a "company man"? As I have said, some bosses prefer their advisors to be company men, but sometimes it's necessary to man-up and tell the boss what he needs to hear—not just what he wants to hear—especially when the consequences of not doing so are serious. Consider the atmosphere of the Bush White House during the buildup to the second Iraq War.

George Tenet was CIA director on September 11, 2001, and he was one of the main reasons the United States invaded Iraq. It was Tenet's job to gather and analyze raw intelligence and then make recommendations to the president about what the intelligence meant. Analyzing raw intelligence is notoriously difficult for many reasons. It's been described as being like reading a map from across a dimly lit room with sunglasses on. Anyone who handles raw intelligence will tell you it's often difficult to establish firm conclusions. Nonetheless, the pressure to go to war was so great that it clouded Tenet's judgment and led him to unwisely advise the president that war with Iraq was justified and necessary.

He famously described the evidence suggesting that Iraq possessed weapons of mass destruction as a "slam dunk." It became clear years later that the intelligence was not the "slam dunk" that Tenet said it was. But it helped to encourage the president, who was hell-bent on going to war, and his cabinet members quickly realized that war with Iraq was inevitable. Tenet felt pressure to do his part, so he presented the president with the erroneous interpretation that Iraq possessed weapons of mass destruction. And so, the war began.

As you may know, Bush's secretary of state, Colin Powell, was also caught up in the company-man mentality at the White House during the buildup to the war. Despite his reservations, Powell bowed to the pressure and fell into lockstep with the administration. Not only did doing so permanently damage the gold-plated reputation that he had built up over two decades in Washington, his participation significantly influenced the decisions of other countries to join the war effort.

As a young staffer, you will probably not be in a position to advise the boss on anything more serious than where to stand during a photo op, or which street to take on the way to an event, but eventually every staffer must face the decision of what sort of advisor he should be. The boss's preferred method for being advised will set the tone of the office. But as Tenet's life illustrates, there are times when events may require you to deviate from the boss's preference. It's better to struggle with the question of what type of advisor you want to be now when the consequences of your decisions are relatively minor, rather than to wait to decide when the consequences are grave and the world hangs on the decision.

Managing the Ego

A big part of working for a prince is managing his colossal ego. Imagine the kind of ego it takes to run for public office: a politician at his core is a person who believes that he alone, out of hundreds or hundreds of thousands or millions or even hundreds of millions of people, is the best qualified and most capable person to do that job. Imagine the kind of ego that would have to exist for a person to think that way. Every time you approach your boss you must be mindful that his ego drives him and you need to treat him accordingly. For example, you must always remember that no matter how friendly or personable your boss may be, and no matter how many times he insists that you call him by his first name and not by his title, he secretly wants you and everyone else to refer to him by the title of his office.

He does not work all those long hours in a relatively low paying job just so people can call him Bob and think he's one of guys. He didn't run for office to be one of the guys! This might seem like an obvious point, especially in light of what I have been saying all this time about how insecure some politicians can be, but politicians don't want to be treated like ordinary people.

Your job as a staffer is always to be mindful of his insecurities and the ego that propelled him to seek elected office. Always treat him with respect, especially when in public. That means, if he is a congressman, call him congressman—if he is a councilman, call him councilman. Whenever you see the president of the United States speak, the seal of his office is always on the podium. When you see the president at a public function, the royal blue and gold trimmed presidential flag is always nearby, and when he enters the room, "Hail to the Chief" is playing. These symbols are not intended to remind you who he is. You know who he is! These symbols of his presidency are intended to *remind him* that you know he is the president, and that he is in charge. A congressman or a senator or a city councilman doesn't have a flag or a great seal or a presidential limousine—but he does have you.

Remembering small details, like calling him by his official title, emphasize for him that you recognize his power and you acknowledge all the work he put into getting elected. If you insist on treating him like one of the guys, even if he seems to want it, he will secretly resent you for it.

Influencing a Prince

When dealing with the prince, you want him to always go away with the impression that you are bending every sinew to the task of serving him. You want him thinking that you rise in the morning and lay down your head at night with thoughts dancing in your brain of ways to make his life better. You want to develop a reputation for willingly and eagerly executing any task required of you, no matter how meager or exalted, with energy and commitment. Achieving this will help secure you a place among those he values, and it will increase your chances of surviving in politics. But there is another equally important thing you can do that can make you even more valuable, even indispensible, in his eyes—develop your own outside resources that you can put at his service.

These resources can be any number of things that are of value to the established prince or the person seeking elected office—access to money or access to people with money, access to votes or just being able to deliver bodies to an event when attendance is important.

All of these things are important to elected officials because money and people are the foundation upon which political campaigns are built. If you can reliably provide any one of these resources to your boss when he needs it, you increase your stock with him—and by extension—you possess the tools to put pressure on him if you want something.

Being a good advisor makes you a valuable resource to your boss. But advisors, even good advisors, are a dime a dozen, and this status is not a guarantee that you will survive in politics. Being able to produce your own resources to help your boss get elected or reelected will raise you above the status of valuable to indispensable. Walking in the door with your own constituency makes you bulletproof.

There are so many people employed in politics today who are there not because they are the best qualified person for the job, but because they walked into the interview with a list of valuable resources they could deliver to the prince. These "political deliverables" are a source of indisputable power to a courtier.

During Machiavelli's day, you were valuable to a prince if you could raise an army on his behalf. Today it's no different. If you can raise an army of volunteers or an army of funders, you are just as valuable.

Consider the great builder and urban planner Robert Moses. If Moses were alive today he could say with complete confidence that no other single human being is more responsible for what the city of New York is and will be for centuries to come. For decades, this one man personally signed off on every bridge, highway, sewer, beach, school, and park built in the New York metro area. This unelected government bureaucrat, who had to be appointed to the commissions on which he served, was more powerful than many of the princes he worked under because of the considerable resources he possessed and could put at their disposal if he chose to.

Moses's power rivaled that of governors and New York City mayors because he built a political and financial machine so formidable that no politician dared challenge him directly. The resources at his disposal enabled him to destroy any elected or appointed official in the state who stood in his way.

As the city's chief builder and planner, Moses used tolls and fees collected from bridges and highways and construction projects to provide "legal" payoffs to politicians in the form of attorney's fees and public relations retainers. He did this so effectively that almost every elected official in the city owed him a favor. He also used the funds to finance an information-gathering machine that he used to blackmail anyone he couldn't bribe. He used the power and influence he established to build what we know today as New York. When Jay-Z describes the "Empire State" in his music it's Moses's creation that he is talking about: a city of breathtaking immensity, with majestic shoulders where anything is possible and where everything is a matter of life and death. If you drive or live or work in New York City or in one the boroughs, you are surrounded by examples of the driving ambition and unadulterated power of Robert Moses.[8]

I'm not recommending that you aspire to being Moses, who was a fascinating but morally flawed man, whose actions did as much to harm New Yorkers as they did to help them. But his life is worthy of study because it provides an important illustration of how to achieve longevity in politics. Over the course of his almost fifty-year career, Moses worked for a dozen different mayors and governors, and he grew more powerful with each new administration. He did so because he brought his own resources to the table. He didn't bet all his chips on one prince, or hitch his fate to someone else's star, hoping that would make him indirectly powerful. Instead, he used his position to accumulate his own power and used that to influence the prince.

You may not be able to produce on the scale that Moses could, but you can build your own reliable network of resources—whether they be financial or otherwise. By doing so, you make yourself valuable to your boss in a way that others among his advisors cannot. And you dramatically increase your chances of political survival.

You are early in your career and probably believe that there is little you can bring to the table at this point. That is not true. There are three things that politicians need most: votes, money, and campaign volunteers. Even you can help provide these resources. If you have friends, then you have access to a potential source of votes or volunteers for your boss. If you have family and they have friends, then you have access to a source of fund-raising potential. All you have to do is figure out how to organize them—which won't be difficult because your friends and family love you and will want to help you. So, make a list of your friends and family and figure out who is most willing to donate a few dollars to your boss's campaign or who is more willing to come join you in a day of door knocking or phone banking for the boss. Anyone, even an intern, can mobilize these resources.

I remember getting some great advice from a former state senator once during the early days of my career about how to fund-raise even if you don't have a lot of money. She told me that when she first got started in politics, she didn't have much money to donate to the local political party system. She realized that all she could really do was save up and regularly donate a small amount every month. She did that consistently for years. Eventually, the regularity of the donations was noticed and she was invited to political party events as a result. She got to know people and those people eventually helped her run for office. I realized that even though I didn't have much money at the time, I could do the same for my boss. In the beginning, it was not much more than a week's worth of beer money, but the regularity of that $25 each month did not go unnoticed. You should combine a regular campaign donation with regular campaign volunteering. Campaigns always need volunteers. And you don't actually have to work for your boss's campaign to get credit. You can get advice from him about which other political candidates he supports, and if he doesn't need you to help him, you could go volunteer for them instead. If you do a good job, that candidate will indentify you with your boss and your boss will remember the favor.

There are many campaign related things you can—and should—do, even at this early point in your career, to raise your status with your boss. And you don't have to do things on a Robert Moses scale to get noticed. Even small things done on a consistent basis will help.

PART TWO

THE AMERICAN COURTIER

5 | ON BEING A COURTIER

In Courts there seems to be a tempest that drives those who are most favored by their lords and they are raised from the humblest condition to the most exalted.

—Castiglione

The Life

It was late and as usual about this time, I had my head between my legs. There was a series of late votes on the State Department reauthorization bill and, since I was the foreign affairs guy in the office, I was the only one who had to stay monitoring the floor proceedings on the office television. Everyone else had gone home long ago. I was doing what I always did before I left for the evening. I had just finished tying the first shoe and was reaching for the second when I noticed on the screen a member whose name escapes me standing at the podium on the Senate floor. The chamber was empty except for him, the clerk, and a stenographer. The only reason I looked up at all was because his voice broke.

He had come to the floor to report that his chief of staff had died at her desk earlier that day of a heart attack. An intern found her slumped over her keyboard with her eyes still open. No one had noticed. Her office was at the end of the hall, so if you looked in at her through the glass, she looked as if she might be sleeping.

She was forty-six years old. She came to Congress in the 1980s as an intern and stayed. She was recently named by the Capitol Hill publication Roll Call *to its list of the "Fabulous Fifty" staff members for "her savvy, her clout, and her access to powerful people."*

"It is with profound sadness that I announce the passing of my chief of staff," said the senator. "She died suddenly today. I cannot express the sorrow and shock I am dealing with in the wake of such a stunning loss. She was a trusted aide, a dear friend, a tireless worker, and a rabid Yankees fan."

I didn't really know her, but we had met once outside the Senate Chamber while waiting for our bosses. I noticed she smelled like baby powder and cigarettes and she wore one of those wraparound dresses I like, with the sash that loops through and around like a belt. She was still a relatively young woman in the middle of her career. She left behind no family—her job was literally her life and death.

I was still fairly new to Capitol Hill at the time, and I was feeling overwhelmed by the frantic pace. No day would end without me having to break into a full-bore run at some point. Two committee hearings a day; hourly meetings; bills to track on the floor; recommendations to make; statements to write—I was rushing the minute I arrived in the morning until I left at night. I can't even count the number of times I said to myself that the job will kill me— and I wasn't some middle-aged lifer; I was a kid. Here I was sitting alone in a dark office late at night, watching in silence as a member of Congress, standing in an empty chamber, told the life story of someone whose life was not that much different than my own. Suddenly, the future didn't seem so bright.

"A Tempest Drives Those Who Are Most Favored by Their Lords and THEY Are Raised from the Humblest Condition to the Most Exalted."

Staff heart attacks on Capitol Hill are rare, but not unheard of. Years of bad food, too much coffee, and the frenetic tempo wear the body down and eventually something has to give. Like any other job, a life in politics has its good and bad aspects, but politics also has elements that make it unlike any other profession and often worth all its challenges.

Castiglione's quote describes one of the benefits of being a courtier. In politics, serving a prince enables a courtier to develop a personal relationship with him that someone else who doesn't have as frequent contact cannot.

The courtier's close proximity to the prince often aids the courtier's professional advancement. Princes tend to surround themselves with advisors they like and are comfortable with. When a position opens on his staff, he is more likely to fill that post with someone he knows rather than someone he doesn't, even if that person is not perfectly qualified for the post. Working closely with the prince helps to cement a courtier's relationship with him and, if the relationship is a good one, can lead to further opportunities down the line. Another way to build a relationship with the prince is during a political campaign—when staffs are smaller and work more closely together. Given the many social elements of political campaigns, it is a good opportunity to see a prince in a more relaxed mood than one might ordinarily see in a working environment. The more relaxed environment means greater potential to actually get to know him and of him getting to know you. Another great thing about campaigns is that they afford people much farther down the ranks the opportunity to cross paths with the prince in a meaningful way.

I remember volunteering on my first campaign and, after having been there only a couple of weeks, being assigned the task of bringing in coffee to the governor as he made fund-raising calls in the tiny private office he used for that purpose. I was completely new to politics and was scared to death of having to bring the governor of my state—a man I had voted for—coffee each afternoon. It was amazing! For five minutes a couple days a week it was the governor and me alone! He hated making fund-raising calls and after he got to know me, we would chat about it. I was still in college at the time and the opportunity to get to know personally the governor of my state was not an opportunity that would have come to me unless I had worked on his campaign. When he won, I was offered a job working in his orbit at the State House, where I continued to run into him from time to time. I would not have gotten that job if I hadn't gotten to know him personally by bringing him coffee during that campaign.

Swift advancement is just one characteristic of court life that at times can be fun, exciting, and professionally satisfying, and at other times demoralizing, exhausting, and embittering—here are a few reasons why.

The Good

Any way you cut it, court life favors the young. The modern day court, whether it be at the White House or the US Capitol or the State House, is a fast-paced, adrenaline-fueled world where even the most innocuous event can suddenly snowball into a national crisis. Such an environment eventually wears on the nerves of the wise and experienced, and they move on. But their absence creates a wealth of opportunities for the young and unencumbered.

Those TV images of Jake Sullivan-like wunderkinds, with floppy hair and baggy suits running the State Department, are not as farfetched as they might seem. In state houses, city councils, and on Capitol Hill, the halls are buzzing with the energy of the young. And some of them are pretty powerful. Because of the nature of politics and politicians, power is not really that difficult to achieve for a courtier.

In politics, it's the staffers, not the politicians, who handle much of the details of the day-to-day work. In some cases, they do all of the work. You'll remember from civics class the stories of how the feathery-light management style of President Ronald Reagan created a power vacuum in the White House that was filled by a trio of staffers who ended up running the country during his first term. Or maybe you've heard in history class about how the young Henry VIII hated the daily work of governing so much that he was happy to have his chief secretaries Cardinal Wolsey and Thomas Cromwell run the country for him while he went off in search of more stimulating amusements elsewhere.

More impressively, maybe you've heard of perhaps the greatest courtier of them all, Don Ruy Gomez de Silva, who was the childhood friend and chief aide of Phillip II of Spain in the sixteenth century. King Phillip was next in line to be Holy Roman Emperor, which in those days meant you pretty much ran the world. But in the early days of his reign, Phillip's insecurities about being king and his willingness to delegate authority to aides combined to help Gomez accumulate a level of influence almost unmatched since then. If Gomez was alive today, he would be the equivalent of a twenty-one-year-old White House chief of staff.

In some professions, youth is a disadvantage. In politics, youth neither hurts you nor helps you. If you can do the work, it almost doesn't matter how old you are, and the power and influence you build can be deployed for modest effects, like helping someone who's lost his job, or for more dramatic purposes like the time I worked with the State Department, the national media, and human rights groups to help free an activist from an Iranian prison. The ease of achieving power and the good you can do with it is just one aspect of why being a staffer is such satisfying work—and there are many more.

The Theatrical Rush

Politics is a lot like being on stage, and it's not just your prince who has a chance to perform. Whether it's at a political rally or a fund-raiser or when constituents come by the office to visit, I find myself almost daily in the presence of an audience. The energy of being on stage is even more tangible if I have to attend a committee hearing with my boss.

Ordinary hearings in the state Senate are not that much different than hearings in the US Senate. They are mostly somber affairs. But occasionally, they turn into spectacles. After ten years and over five hundred hearings, I still get a little nervous before walking into a hearing room—much like I imagine an actor does before walking out on stage.

The world of politics is glamorous. I've traded small talk with Bill Gates, shared a bag of peanuts with the world-wide chairman of Toyota, and waited for an elevator with the biggest rock star on the planet. My job has also enabled me to travel the globe. In fact, I'm writing these lines from a Tel Aviv hotel room overlooking the Mediterranean, where I'm visiting as part of a congressional staff delegation. As a foreign policy staffer to a member of Congress, I travel more than I ever do in private life. And as a government staffer, traveling as a guest of a foreign nation, I travel in style.

The first time I flew first class was on a congressional trip. I watched the sunset from the top of the Great Wall of China on a congressional trip; I slept in marble-lined luxury in the Winter Palace in Luxor, Egypt, with a balcony the size of most apartments overlooking the Nile; and I took my first sip of expensive champagne while sitting in a sidewalk café on the West Bank in Paris while on a congressional staff trip. If you want to see the world, you can join the military and see it on a soldier's salary, or you can become a congressional staffer and see it in style. You choose.

The Historical Brush

In many ways, being a policy staffer is like being a lawyer or even a teacher because of the meaningful and lasting ways you are able to impact the lives of ordinary people. If you work in the personal office of an elected official, for example, as opposed to being a committee staffer, where contact with constituents is rare, a significant portion of your day is consumed by responding to constituent concerns. These concerns can be as pedestrian as helping someone get their electricity restored after a storm or as complex as drafting legislation that changes the tax code. And unlike being an investment banker, who may never personally witness the immediate effects of his actions or decisions on the lives of those he helps, being a political staffer offers you a chance to see almost immediately the consequences of your efforts.

While success in getting a constituent's lights turned back on can be intoxicating stuff for some staffers, the most potent aspect of a staffer's influence is his ability to make laws that influence lives and impact history. Of course, it's the elected official's job to make policy, but most politicians don't have the time to do anything more than provide the broad strokes of an idea to a staffer who does the rest. Being a staffer gives you a chance to play a key role in your boss's policy making and might even give you a chance to make history. American history books are filled with stories of staffers who, after being given free reign by their bosses, went on to do extraordinary things.

Consider Benjamin Franklin. During the American Revolution, Franklin was sent as an envoy to the court of Louis XVI to secure France's support in America's war against the British. Though France and Great Britain were enemies and had fought a succession of bloody battles with each other for dominance of the seas, coming to the aid of the American revolutionaries was not a particularly attractive proposition for the French. First, the United States was only in its infancy and had little to offer that France did not already possess. Also, the Americans at this time were still an unknown quantity and had presented few firm indications that they had the capacity to defeat the British. Further, the French nobility was facing its own social and civil pressures, which support of the Americans could, and would, inflame. Coming to our aid could exacerbate already-strained tensions between these two imperial powers and draw the French into an expensive and protracted conflict.

Despite all of this and with few resources other than his personal charm and intelligence, Franklin convinced France to grant aid and military support to the Americans. This extraordinary gesture was leveraged by the Americans to get support and financing from other countries and became one of the chief reasons we won the war. By doing the impossible and securing French support, Franklin achieved one of the greatest, if not *the* greatest, foreign policy successes this country has ever known. At some point, every staffer who is engaged in policy making has a chance to play a role in history. All you have to do is get into the arena.[9]

The Vocational Push

The biggest advantage of being in politics is the boost it can give your career. There are many reasons for this.

Foremost is the close working relationship that staffers have with decision makers. When the time comes for politicians to appoint a person to a vital post on their team, they rarely choose a person they have no relationship with. They often choose friends, or others with whom they have formed good working partnerships throughout their careers. When President George W. Bush was elected president and needed a national security advisor, he gave the job to Condoleezza Rice, who was a good family friend and who had been his foreign policy advisor during the campaign. When the post of secretary of state was vacated during his second term, he asked Rice to fill that slot as well.

When Elizabeth I became queen, she picked as her principal advisor and chief secretary Lord Burghley, a man who was responsible for overseeing the maintenance of one of her country homes. When President George Washington needed a treasury secretary, he chose Alexander Hamilton, the man who had been his aide-de-camp during the Revolutionary War. You don't have to start in a high-ranking position to rise either. The history books are filled with examples of how the mere proximity to power propelled mediocre careers into the stratosphere almost overnight.

Before he became President Truman's "fix-it guy," Clark Clifford had been a well-regarded and popular lawyer in his home town of St. Louis, Missouri. He started working for Truman in the very minor post of assistant to the president's naval advisor, but within only a couple of years he rose to become a national figure. After recognizing Truman's lack of experience and insecurity in office and the dearth of talented and effective advisors around him, Clifford used the proximity of his largely ceremonial naval post as a platform to showcase his many talents. His talents were recognized quickly and he soon rose to become one of Truman's principal advisors. Eventually, not long after joining the administration, Clifford became what we today refer to as the national security advisor, a role that did not exist before him.

Years later, Henry Kissinger became national security advisor to President Richard Nixon and transformed himself into the most powerful national security advisor the country had ever known. Part of this was luck. Kissinger had worked for presidents Kennedy and Johnson in lesser policy positions. When President Nixon came to office determined to control all aspects of foreign policy making in the White House, he recognized that he needed to neutralize the influence of the defense and state departments. The reconsolidation of power and the turf battles that would have to be fought between the

White House and the state and defense departments to achieve it would require the leadership of an extraordinary person. He would need to possess a high degree of paranoia and a superior ability to deceive others. Nixon recognized these qualities in Kissinger. When the secretary of state eventually grew tired of being shut out by Kissinger and Nixon and resigned, Kissinger took his job. Kissinger went on to be a celebrated secretary of state and a Nobel Laureate—all in the span of six years—jumping over perhaps dozens of people more qualified for the post than he was.

The Cush

Finally, being a staffer is a good way to get rich . . . eventually. Thomas Jefferson is legendary for having died deep in debt after devoting much of his life to public service. His family had to sell most of his possessions, even Monticello, to get out from under the massive debts he accumulated over the course of his long life. But his debts were more about the result of poor choices than earning potential. The most valuable asset a former staffer possesses, in addition to his policy expertise, his institutional knowledge, and his political instincts, is his collection of relationships. Companies, institutions, and even governments will pay you handsomely for your insights into the thinking and decision making of your former bosses and for your ability to fill a room with your former colleagues. After a life of exhausting and low-paying work to advance someone else's career, it's nice to know there is a soft landing waiting for you at the end.

I was a staffer in Congress the year my party gained control of the House of Representatives. A change in political leadership is often accompanied by a shift at lobbying firms as they try to hire new staffers to match the new party in power who can help them gain the access they need to influence these policy makers. The salaries they offer to attract these staffers can be considerable. A friend invited me to lunch a few weeks after the election and told me that someone with my years of experience and political connections could make as much as $200,000 a year as a lobbyist. I wasn't shocked because I had a friend who had just accepted a job as a political strategist for an international bank making twice that much. And you don't have to work as a lobbyist at the federal level to make this kind of money. Lobbyists at the state level can also make six-figure salaries. If you put in your time, make a lot of friends, and develop some policy expertise, you too can have access to this kind of money when you are ready to leave government service.

The Bad & The Ugly

The Hours & Pay

Regardless of whether you work in a state capitol, for a city councilman, or for a US congressman, the tenure of most staffers is relatively short. On Capitol Hill, for instance, few staffers remain on The Hill longer than a few years. Long hours and low pay are the chief reasons for this. Let me pause for a second and unpack what I mean when I say "long hours" for those of you among the truly uninitiated. When I say long hours, I mean ridiculously long hours— "finals week" hours. Imagine working the kinds of hours you did during finals week in college on a daily basis. Ten, eleven, fourteen hour days—every day. As ridiculous as that sounds, there are staffers on Capitol Hill who have worked these kinds of hours for years, even decades.

If you're low down on the ladder, you might be spared some of this, but you can count on long hours if you hold a leadership post because you will be on call twenty-four hours a day. I got my first taste of how long the hours could be when in college I was a White House intern. One day it dawned on me that there was so much to do that a White House staffer could literally work twenty-four hours straight every day and still not get everything done. I came to Capitol Hill hoping the hours would be a little better, but they were no different. There are hearings and votes to prepare your boss for, constituent complaints to address, meetings to attend—both yours and your boss's— and a never ending stack of reading to be done and letters to write.

And then there's the pay—which is sad. Most staffers who commit to long-term service eventually must come to terms with the trade-off where salary is concerned. The lower you are in the office hierarchy, the lower your pay.

On the lowest rungs, the salary is barely enough to live on. On the highest rungs, the salaries are decent, though nowhere near comparable to what can be made in the private sector.

The Job Insecurity

Then there's the job insecurity. Most elected officials run for reelection every four years. In the US House of Representatives, it's every two years, and in the US Senate, it's every six years. As I said earlier, every elected official is vulnerable to being unseated—regardless of how powerful he is. If the elected official loses office, often the staffer is out of a job too. I've been in that position, but I was lucky; I didn't have a family or a mortgage, so I could afford to be out of work while I looked for another job. Even if you are fortunate enough to have no dependents, when you lose your job, it's never a good feeling. Every longtime political staffer has faced this situation at least once.

Five hundred years ago, during the turbulent period between the reigns of Henry VIII and Elizabeth I of England, there was a young and gifted staffer named William Cecil, whose career was abruptly brought to an end when his boss was accused of treason and sent to the Tower of London.

According to Cecil, this event was the single most instructive of his early professional life. His boss, the Duke of Somerset, de facto ruler of England at the time, was thrown into the Tower because his fellow dukes had grown tired of his heavy-handed leadership. To get rid of him, they falsely accused him of treason and began the legal process of separating his head from the rest of his body. As Somerset's devoted servant, Cecil was thrown into the Tower with him. While Somerset alone was the cause of his downfall and eventual death, the twenty-nine-year old Cecil, by his unfortunate connection to Somerset, might have suffered the same fate as his boss. He survived though and was released. Eventually he became one of England's greatest courtiers and was elevated to the title of Lord Burghley when Elizabeth I ascended to the throne. But the experience taught him a valuable lesson about the instability of life at court.[10]

A staffer can lose his job as a result of a major event or a minor one. Think about the fate of all the staffers who worked for Richard Nixon in his final days. Remember Nixon's infamous White House tapes? Well, the machines that recorded the incriminating evidence that was used to force Nixon to resign were originally installed because Nixon was jealous of all the media attention Henry Kissinger was getting. Nixon innocently had the recording devices installed in order to build a historical record that it was he, not Kissinger, who was the foreign policy genius in the White House. In other words, Nixon's own insecurities led him to take a seemingly reasonable course of action that ultimately secured his own downfall. And when he went down, a lot of gifted, dedicated public servants went down with him.

... and the Unhealthy Lifestyle

Don't let yourself become like most staffers who survive the long hours and job insecurity only to be brought down by the bad food and stress. It doesn't have to happen. Unless the job is making you fabulously rich, or you are saving someone's life, no job is worth ruining your health over. It is so easy for this to happen in politics that you need to consider making a pact with yourself early on that you will not let it happen to you. You are no good to anyone— not your boss, not your family, no one, if you kill yourself trying to attach an amendment to a transportation bill. Besides, the healthier you are, the more you can get done. You may think that you are too young to be thinking about this now, but I'm here to tell you, you are not.

I was lucky. Seeing that member of Congress standing on the Senate floor, giving a speech about the death of his staffer, scared me just enough to make me determined that it would not happen to me. I resolved to always eat well and take care of myself. After more than a decade in politics, I've watched as friends of mine have let the job ruin their health. Watching that senator give that speech may have saved my life.

6 | ON THE QUALITIES AND SKILLS OF SUCCESSFUL COURTIERS

*The Ideal Courtier should practice in
everything a certain nonchalance that
shall conceal design and show that what is
done and said is done without effort and
almost without thought.*

—Castiglione

For a second, Clark Clifford stopped breathing. The president had asked everyone to take their seats, but as Harry Truman settled into his chair, he looked up to find Clifford and Secretary of State George Marshall still standing. Clifford had hoped to take his usual place next to the president, but Marshall was blocking his path, silently challenging Clifford to step aside. As the puzzled spectators looked on, five seconds passed as the two men stood motionless. Then, Clifford moved slightly to his left to surrender the chair, but as he did so, Marshall, without lowering his gaze, moved with him. Suddenly, as if responding to a signal audible only to him, Marshall's eyes softened and he stepped aside. Still a little confused, Clifford settled into the only other remaining seat in the room as Marshall lowered himself into the chair next to the president.

Marshall didn't like Clifford, who he suspected of using his influence with the president to convince him to support Israel's bid for independence. Not only was Marshall upset about Clifford delving into his territory as secretary of state, he thought Clifford's actions were motivated not with the nation's foreign policy in mind, but purely in an effort to win the Jewish vote in the upcoming election.

The president called the meeting to order and invited Marshall to go first. Truman had assembled his foreign policy staff to discuss Marshall's opposition to Truman's decision to recognize the State of Israel. Since Clifford was not a member of the international affairs team, Truman's decision to invite him only confirmed in Marshall's mind Clifford's role in the president's controversial decision. Revealing his agitation, Marshall addressed his presentation not to the president, but to Clifford. Marshall's position was already well known to everyone, so his presentation was brief. When he finished, he looked over at Truman. Truman then gave Clifford the floor.

Everyone turned to find Clifford sitting perfectly still and erect with his palms pressed before him and his thumbs stacked as if in prayer. He waited for complete silence. When everyone's eyes were squarely on him—he began.

The sound of his voice was sonorous and ringing like an echo in a cave. He spoke slowly and carefully, fully enunciating each syllable as he went as if each one was a separate and distinct entity. The words vibrated deep inside his chest, rose up, and with invisible strength issued forth like an invitation delivered a word at a time until its full meaning emerged.

Truman was familiar with Clifford's technique, but the others were not. The president studied their faces closely as they sat transfixed. Clifford spoke for a half-hour, addressing each of Marshall's criticisms in turn, with a logical and thorough cascade of evidence. Each point punctuated with a perfectly placed hand gesture and the faintest hint of a self-satisfied smile. And then, as suddenly as he began, he stopped. The sound of an ice cube cracking in a glass on the table broke the spell.

"The Ideal Courtier Should Practice in Everything a Certain Nonchalance That Shall Conceal Design and Show That What Is Done and Said Is Done without Effort and almost without Thought."

If Castiglione were observing this scene, he would applaud Clifford's undeniable skill as a captivating communicator, and he would recommend that you strive to achieve a similar level of skill.

Clifford's presentation style was often described as mesmerizing and effortless by the people who witnessed it. This style had made Clifford one of the most successful lawyers in St. Louis, and he often used it whenever the stakes were highest and he needed to be his most per-suasive. It may have been mesmerizing, but it was hardly effortless. Often before Clifford had to make an important presentation, he would rise early and go to the spare bed-room where he kept the standing mirror he used to prac-tice his important speeches. He would study the outline of his speech over and over until every word and point was committed to memory. Then he turned his attention to the presentation, experimenting with different styles and emphasizing different words and phrasing to develop the optimal desired effect. Clifford's purpose was always to persuade you *completely*—and he almost always succeeded. Though the task required long hours of practice and prepa-ration, the effect was undeniable.[11]

Castiglione provides a long, though dated, list of skills and qualities the ideal courtier should possess. Some of them are relevant to today's courtier and others are not, but one in particular deserves your close attention—the idea of being so good at something that the action appears effortless.

Castiglione says that where skill is concerned, courtiers should strive to achieve mastery to the point of artistry.

In *The Book of the Courtier* he discusses the issue in the context of describing the effortlessness of the most skilled Renaissance soldiers, but the same concept can apply to Clifford's seemingly effortless skill as a communicator. Truman valued Clifford's advice, but he admired and grew to rely on Clifford's abilities as a communicator more. I am encouraging you to follow Castiglione's advice, and try to raise the level of your skills to artistry—but not for the reason you might think.

If you haven't already noticed, one of the main messages of this book is that, as a staffer, your number one goal should always be to survive. You cannot be a public servant if you don't have a job. Survival is often about reinforcing your value to the prince and standing out from among your peers. Presenting a front of effortlessness in the areas that count is a way to do just that. You understand of course from the Clifford illustration that this approach requires a lot of work. But the rewards are potentially limitless.

If you know anything about Clark Clifford, you know he made many mistakes as an advisor—one almost earned him a prison term. But it is for his ability as a communicator, not as an advisor, that I am recommending him to you. Truman assigned Clifford the task of addressing Marshall's concerns because he knew how skilled and persuasive a communicator he was. Clifford's abilities demonstrate an essential element of being a good staffer—being a clear and effective communicator. He was a lawyer by profession and his presentation style was the product of dozens of courtroom trials—many of which he won. You shouldn't expect to exercise the same level of ability at this early point in your career. But remember that communication, like any other skill, can be learned and perfected. Clifford didn't begin his career as a mesmerizing speaker.He taught himself to be one, and there is no reason you can't do the same.

Think back to freshman orientation when you were told that the person on your left and right may not be there four years later. I'm playing that role in your life today. I'm here to tell you that in two years—not four—many of the friends you made on your first day in the office, for a range of reasons, will no longer be there. Many of them will be let go because they don't have the skills to do the job.

Communication is just one skill on a long list of necessary qualities and skills you will need to be a good staffer in politics, including being graceful under pressure, managing coalitions well, being able to speak compellingly while actually saying little, and having good political instincts. If you've already read Castiglione's book, you know which abilities were most prized among Renaissance courtiers. Now let's look at the qualities and skills that are most prized today.

Qualities and Skills All Good Courtiers Must Possess

Every year, hundreds of thousands of people like you descend on city councils and state houses and legislatures across this country looking for a taste of what it's like to work in politics. Most will start as interns. But once their internships are over, the vast majority of them will move on, never to return. Some will discover that they dislike the backslapping fakeness of politics or the pace or sausage-making aspect of policy making. Others will leave because they discover they are simply unprepared for the work.

Like any highly demanding profession, being a good political staffer requires a special array of skills and qualities that not everyone has and a degree of self-knowledge and an intellectual maturity that most people fresh out of college haven't yet developed. I was one of those people. I got fired from my first job as a staffer because I didn't understand how to do the work and because I couldn't adjust fast enough.

There are basically two main types of political staffers: policy wonks and mechanics. When mechanics ask a question, they want the right answer now. The wonks want the right answer now too, but they also want to see your work. Wonks are just as interested in how you got the answer as they are in the answer itself. Mechanics are mostly interested in how the machine works—they are fascinated by the rules and how to use them to get things done. Wonks want to know what the machine is fed, they want to know where you bought the food, and they want command of the spoon. The difference between a mechanic and a wonk can be seen as the difference between being intellectually curious and being an intellectual. Mechanics are really only just interested in the bottom line. I am a mechanic.

When I started, I thought I was a wonk, mostly because people who have no idea what a wonk is told me I was. I remember the moment it hit me that we were all wrong.

I had recently begun a new job as a legislative assistant to a freshman member of Congress. I had never worked on legislation before, and I had never worked on Capitol Hill. I got the job because I happened to have worked with the congressman's chief of staff in my previous job. She liked me and, despite my lack of experience, gave me a chance.

From the very start I knew the job was not right for me. I was drowning. It was like trying to take a drink from a fire hydrant through a paper straw. For the most part, my problem was that I couldn't organize all of the information coming at me. Legislative assistants on Capitol Hill are expected to stay abreast of all the issue areas in their portfolio. Depending on the size of the staff, a person could have as few as five issue areas to cover or as many as fifteen. I had fifteen. I soon discovered that mechanics are not necessarily good jugglers. So, like a classic mechanic, to keep up, I would just jump to the bottom line of an issue and move on. The problem was—the prince I served was a wonk.

Where policy making is concerned, if the wonk is the superhero, the mechanic is his evil nemesis. Wonks like things to be communicated to them a certain way and they tend to ask a lot of questions. Mechanics like to get to the root of things immediately. I had never worked for anyone like him before. Every interaction was an intellectual exercise. He would send me off in search of an answer to a question, and when I returned, he had thought up all new questions. He was obviously smart, and though years of education and the praise of brilliant people had convinced me I was no slouch either, I could never seem to satisfy him.

The end eased up on me softly from behind wearing comfortable flats. I didn't notice anything at first, but issue areas in my portfolio began to be siphoned off by the chief of staff and discreetly assigned to other people in the office. I found that I was spending less and less time with the congressman, and I staffed him at fewer and fewer meetings. Then I began to notice that he had developed a nervous habit of looking at the clock whenever we were alone. One day, the chief of staff invited me to lunch, and slipped in the knife.

If you are serious about being a policy maker, my advice to you is to figure out what type of staffer you are right from the start. Are you intellectually curious with limited interest in ideas, or are you an intellectual with a deep interest in how ideas are generated? Answering this question honestly now will spare you a world of pain later. Only after you have determined how you process information can you then turn your attention to the subject of developing the skills and qualities you will need to be effective. Before reading the next paragraph, take a second, put the book down, and think about how you process information. Seriously.

Welcome back. Now that you have some insight about how you think, to enrich your understanding of the main thrust of the chapter—here are some key skills you need to be able to succeed and survive in politics. After having done this for a while, and having reflected on the thoughts of Machiavelli and Castiglione, I've determined that the best staffers are good communicators, have finely tuned political instincts, are highly sensitive to detail, are graceful under pressure, are observant, and have sophisticated leadership and team-building skills. I also learned that all of these skills and qualities can be learned.

Communication

Writing & Speaking at Court

To be truly useful to your boss you must learn to adapt your style of writing to his. The way it usually works is that a staffer will write a speech in his own style and his boss will edit the text to flow more closely to the way he says things. This process wastes time and eventually all staffers recognize that they can save time and win their boss's trust by learning to mimic his style. Maybe his style is folksy and plain; maybe he likes to use biblical references; maybe he likes to lean heavily on statistics. Your job is to read his past writings and adapt as closely as you can to the way he communicates. But it doesn't end there. Because you work in the world of policy making, you must also learn to write in a style that is general and universally approachable. This is necessary because you will often find yourself having to build a persuasive argument where you cannot hide behind folksy pronouncements and biblical references. You will need to be as cogent, concise, and persuasive as you can without oratorical tricks and gimmicks. For these reasons, all good staffers must be good communicators.

There are two other factors inherent in legislative policy-making, or any political or governance-related advising environment that make having good communication skills essential to the job: the youth and relative inexperience of your fellow staffers and the fast pace of the work.

First, your audience, which includes not just your boss but all of your colleagues, is mostly comprised of recent college grads. Almost all elected officials who are legislators have people on staff to manage the details of legislating. Though this is an important job, it's not one high on the office hierarchy, so the staffer who holds the position is often a person who has only recently graduated from college. If you are lucky, your colleagues will be people who have been around long enough to understand the system. But since the tenure of staffers in legislative bodies is short—on Capitol Hill it's only a couple of years—the odds are you will probably have to work with someone who is new or not very familiar with the process of policy making. To get your message across to these people, you will need to be as clear and as accurate a communicator as possible.

Second, policy making is a complex enterprise made even more difficult by the fast pace of politics, which can often make it hard to gain a deep understanding of issues. Even an ordinary day in politics is a whirlwind of events, and there is rarely adequate time to fully digest issues. So a staffer must be good at quickly distilling a subject to its key elements and then communicating it in a fashion that is easily understood. This is not an easy task.

I can see why communication is one of the first faculties you lose as you age. Think about it: when you communicate with someone, not only must you work to say precisely what it is you mean—which can be difficult even if you have full command of an issue—you must also say it in a way that encourages understanding in the person you are speaking with. Verbal communication, even on the simplest level and face-to-face, is a complicated mental exercise. Communicating in writing is even more of a challenge.

Journalists have the best skill set and communication style for politics. They are often required to distill highly complicated matters into easy-to-understand prose that fit into tightly conscribed news columns. In a quick-paced environment like politics, where your colleagues often lack professional experience or who rarely possess more than a bachelor's degree, a journalist's concise, clear style of communicating is ideal. If you want to be a better communicator, read the paper, especially the op-eds, every day, and try to model your writing on the style of your favorite political journalists.

Being able to distill information to its essential elements is only one-half of the battle, however—you also need to develop a good speaking style that is professional and that inspires confidence. Young, inexperienced people have a tendency to speak too fast. Even though, or because, you are young, you will want to cultivate a professional and mature speaking style that encourages older people to trust you and your views.

Let's go back to Clark Clifford for a second. Throughout his long government career, Clifford built a reputation as an extraordinary communicator. As a lawyer, he could of course be very persuasive, but when you listened to Clifford, it was not just the words that persuaded you, it was also his presentation.

In politics you will encounter many young staffers who will try to overwhelm you with a "wall of words," thinking that a fast-talking presentation style communicates command of the issue and confidence, but a presentation style that is slow and deliberate can be even more persuasive. It was this type of communication style that Clifford built his reputation on.

If Clifford wanted to persuade you, he wouldn't try and hit you with a "wall of words" the way a nervous or inexperienced presenter might. He would speak calmly, slowly, carefully, and clearly. He used this method to minimize distractions around himself and to focus people's attention on his words and the substance of what he was saying. In short, Clifford treated words like currency, and if you want to be seen as a good communicator in politics, you should too. One of his contemporaries described Clifford's speaking style:

"The Clifford manner is deliberate, sonorous, eloquent, and quite un-interruptible. It gathers momentum as it proceeds, and soon achieves a certain mesmerizing effect."

To be successful at this type of speaking, you will need to gather your thoughts in advance, and you will need to develop the confidence to have your voice be the only sound in the room. Speaking calmly and deliberately conveys maturity and confidence—just the qualities you want to display if you want people to look past your youth and focus on your ideas.

Brevity, Silence & Listening

Politics is a verbal profession—and words a politician's toolkit, pallet, and meal ticket. Given this, politics is a field where people can have a tendency to talk too much and listen too little. You will be surrounded by people who will talk only to hear themselves talk or who will talk because they feel they are obliged to. You must avoid this temptation because it ultimately will not serve you well and could threaten your reputation. Talking for the sake of talking, without contributing anything useful to the discussion, will cause people to secretly resent you, suspect you of being vain, or disrespect you. If you are trying to make a good impression, this is not the way to do it.

Yet I'm not saying to sit in the corner silently either. Meetings are an opportunity to make a good impression. Even as an inexperienced staffer, you can make a significant contribution to the discussion and make yourself look good if you listen carefully and focus your efforts on extracting clarifications from the person who is speaking. This approach will make you look much better than asking a question merely for the sake of being heard. It will make you appear engaged and focused.

One thing you can do while helping to clarify the speaker's presentation is to strive to help him or her make his or her point. This technique will make you look like a team player while making you also appear engaged with the conversation. But in order to do this, you will need to follow the discussion carefully.

It's much more impressive to be seen as a keen listener than a selfish speaker. Listen carefully and base your contributions to the conversation on clarifying your understanding of what you hear in a supportive way. I remember once being in a meeting with a room full of senior congressional staff during a discussion about something that I knew nothing about. I listened very carefully to the presentation, and I asked questions to clarify details that I didn't understand. By listening actively and attentively, I was able to nod in all the right places and smile when they smiled and laugh when they laughed. When it was over, my boss asked how it was that I was so familiar with the subject. I told him I knew nothing about the subject. If I seemed to, it was only because I was listening very carefully.

Sir Walter Raleigh, a favorite of Queen Elizabeth I, once said that verbosity is a sign of vanity. He would caution others to listen carefully and speak little because they would be judged harshly for what they did say. He believed that words were dangerous and so powerful that a poorly chosen word could make a courtier a permanent enemy.

Talleyrand was known as a great conversationalist, but he was not a great talker. He actually said very little. He listened carefully so when his turn came to speak, he was always able to say the right thing. His rule was to listen attentively regardless of whether he already knew the information. He was perhaps the most skilled foreign minister of his day, and he thought silence was his cardinal diplomatic weapon. He thought the key was not to come up with the cleverest response, but the right response. This can work for you too. But to do this successfully, you must be willing to listen carefully. If you listen well enough, and struggle to understand what you hear, you will always have something useful to contribute to the conversation.

Speaking without Saying

Despite the title, this section is not about how to lie. It's about how to bob-and-weave during difficult conversations. Though in politics lying is sometimes necessary, and you should be able to do so convincingly, it is not the subject of this chapter or this book. I will, however, say a few words about how to talk around an issue, which I'll save until the end. Let's start with the basics.

Working for an elected official often means having to speak for him. No one is spared this—not even the intern answering phones on his or her first day. You will be asked to speak for your boss regularly, and you should be able to do so compellingly, convincingly, and confidently.

During the early days of the Afghanistan and Iraq wars, a group of constituents decided to hold a vigil in our office protesting my boss's support for war funding. About twenty loud, middle-aged, ponytail wearing, peace-sign flashing, angry husbands, wives, mothers, and fathers descended on our Capitol Hill office without an invitation, their heads probably swirling with memories of the '60s, threatening to launch a sit-in in the middle of our office if the member of Congress did not show himself and explain why he had voted twice to fund the wars. It was a Monday. Since no votes were scheduled, my boss was out of the office attending a school opening in his district.

The crowd got so boisterous and demanding that they had the eighteen-year-old male office assistant at the front desk in tears before the chief of staff asked me to address the group—the war was part of my policy portfolio.

A lot goes through a staffer's mind when faced with a situation where he must speak for his boss. I can still remember standing there, feeling like I was alone on a stage, totally exposed and literally surrounded by hostile constituents demanding answers to questions that I did not have. Would they embarrass me and ask me about some detail of the war that I didn't know? What were my colleagues thinking as they listened to me address this crowd? Were they judging me? How could I get these people to leave?

In the end, I did alright because I had one thing working in my favor—I knew more about the subject than they did. I answered a few softball questions with vague answers and eventually they accepted that my boss really was not in the office and decided to leave.

Reflecting on the scene afterwards, I realized I did some things wrong and some right. Since you are just starting out, you may not end up facing a situation as challenging as the one I just described, but you may find yourself very soon having to respond to the persistent questions of a frustrated constituent. This is what you should do:

First, calm yourself down. Do whatever you have to. You need to be able to think on your feet in situations such as these, and you will not be able to do so if you are flustered, stumbling over your words, or talking too fast. A technique that worked for me in the above situation was to accept who I was and to accept the exposed feeling. All the eyes in the room and all the ears were focused on me—I decided right then and there that I would not care that the hem on one of my pant legs was coming undone and the cuff was dragging on the floor or that my tie had a fresh mustard stain on it or that they might think that I was a little too young to be in that situation. I decided to embrace the exposed feeling and accept my flaws, and that helped calm me down.

Second, get yourself in a professional frame of mind—and stay there. When confronting angry constituents, you need to convey to them that they are being heard. You shouldn't try to brush them off or argue with them. You need to remember that they took the time out of their busy day to call or to come down to the office because they felt strongly about the subject. Remember, these people are not your constituents, they are your boss's. He will not appreciate you doing anything that might lose him a vote. So, you need to be in an open, listening mindset. Even if they are hostile, you should always act professionally, which requires a little preparation. Before taking that call or before walking out to face the angry multitudes, take a deep breath and promise yourself that you will be professional no matter what. I learned that lesson the hard way.

Not long after I had to confront the angry crowd of parents, I was engaged in yet another heated discussion with another group of angry parents about the US relationship with Afghanistan. Fueled by the confidence of their superior numbers, they pressed me combatively in an effort to deliberately break my calm. At one point, one of the parents got personal and asked me how I could be so calm when people were dying. I snapped. A month before, I had to witness the burial at Arlington Cemetery of my closest cousin—a Marine who was killed in Afghanistan. I turned the argument back on them. I asked how many of them had worn the uniform as I had done and how many of them had actually had a close family member in a war. My tone changed from professional to combative. When I was done, I knew I was wrong to have taken the bait. The meeting ended not long after that. One of the parents came up to introduce herself afterwards. She didn't do so to express sympathy with me, but to let me know that she was close to my boss's wife and that she would be informing her of my lack of professionalism. That was the last time I made that mistake. You should always assume that your boss may know the person you are talking to. And assume the conversation will get back to him.

Third, talk only about what you know well enough to speak confidently and compellingly on. You don't want them to go away feeling as if you were bullshitting them. And if you can, try to steer the conversation to issues you are the most familiar with. A bit more about this later.

Fourth, convey empathy. Try to relate to what they are saying. Convey your understanding of their situation by using an illustration from something similar you've experienced. Empathy will help to calm them down by helping them see that you are listening and can relate.

Fifth, the no-brainer: memorize a few key points about how your boss feels on the issues people are talking about. Now, I say no-brainer, but you will be surprised by how few people take the time to actually do this. You think that just because it's your first day as an intern that you won't have to face tough questions about your boss's position? Well, when you call a congressman's office, 80 percent of the time the person who picks up the phone is an intern. When I was working in the White House, I recall that only interns answered the phones. So, ask around about your boss's position on key issues, or review his website for clues about the issues he is writing about and save yourself the embarrassment of getting caught off guard.

Sixth, read the newspaper. There is no way of knowing for sure what the person on the other end of the phone line is going to hit you with, but you can put yourself in the ballpark by reading the paper each morning. Most people who contact their elected official are reacting to something they've read recently in the paper. If you read the paper each day, you will have a leg up.

Seventh, if the question is difficult, remember, you don't have to answer directly or exactly. Answer the question you want to answer regardless of what the question is. If the question is a particularly challenging one, you can ease some of the pressure by answering only that part of the question that you feel most comfortable about answering.

For example, let's say you were on the receiving end of that hostile question I got about my boss's vote to fund the war in Iraq. Let's say your boss, like mine, voted to support funding the war because he supports the troops but not because he supports war in general. You can, like I did, take the issue of supporting the troops and run with it—run like the wind! Talk and talk and talk about how much the troops deserve our support, about how they are doing their duty, about how the United States is a nation built on shared sacrifice.

Finally, a word or two about obfuscation: why it is sometimes necessary to speak without actually saying anything. It all comes down to one thing—the public record. In politics, everything you say and do can someday come back and bite you on the ass. Words are like boomerangs. If you send them out into the world, they always come back.

I remember getting an urgent call once from a constituent who wanted to know in a hurry why it was that my boss was not supporting a certain bill. I remember being suspicious about why he needed to know so quickly. He fired a rapid succession of questions at me. I answered them honestly and calmly. Why hadn't the congressman cosponsored the bill, he asked? I responded that tens of thousands of bills are introduced each year and that no one can be familiar with every single one of them. Fortunately for him, I happened to be familiar with this one.

I discussed the political implications of supporting the bill and discussed the details that the congressman might have found objectionable if he had been informed about the bill and had been talking to the caller. The caller listened attentively and then abruptly excused himself. I thought the whole thing was over, but *twenty minutes* later I got a call from the director of one of the congressman's district offices about a LISTSERV she's on that was slamming my boss for his lack of support for the bill using many of the points I had made on the phone! That's how quickly it can happen. And that's why sometimes you need to be responsive without actually saying anything.

When faced with such a situation, you should be vague and say nothing that can be interpreted negatively. Let them do all the talking. Ask questions—don't give answers. In the case above with the bill, what I should have done was to solicit details about the bill from the caller the way I did when I faced that angry crowd who wanted to stage a sit-in about the war. In that case, I used the opportunity to let them share their views and I asked a lot of questions to diffuse the intensity of the moment.

As an intern or young staffer, the strategy of asking questions can be your most effective defense in a difficult exchange. Don't be afraid to use it.

Coalition Management

Even as an inexperienced staffer, you will find yourself having to exercise leadership over others from time to time. The bulk of your leadership opportunities will probably center on organizing volunteers, such as interns and campaign volunteers, but if you work on legislation, you may find that you will need to exercise leadership over a coalition of groups who are helping you shape policy. You must be able to organize, lead, and manage these policy and political coalitions if you want to be a valued staffer.

First, a word about coalition management on campaigns. If you are involved in politics or even on the margins of politics as an agency employee—or even a lobbyist—you may end up working on a political campaign. You should know that campaigns are fueled by the energy of volunteers. It is not uncommon for a young campaign staffer to have to organize and instruct volunteers, who are often decades older than they are. After only a little experience organizing campaign volunteers you learn they must be treated the way you would young school children: instructions must be spoon fed to them and you have to do as much as you can for them so that they don't have to think too much. Campaign volunteers have daytime jobs, with daytime pressures. They don't volunteer for campaigns because they want to add to those pressures. They want to help, but they don't want to have to think too much about it.

Because of this, campaign staffers need to be loud, self-assured people who have no problem taking charge—think camp counselor. If you are thinking about joining a campaign to get your foot in the door for a policy job, for example, you will need to find those qualities within yourself. If you have already done campaign work and are thinking about getting a job working as a policy maker, you will find that the qualities you need to organize campaign volunteers are not that different from the ones you need to organize political coalitions.

If you work on policy, you will need the support of outside groups to validate your ideas, to advise you, and to help you sell your policy to other policy makers working like you to advance their boss's priorities. Though you may think you are all working together toward the same goal, these groups often have their own agendas, which might not match exactly your own. For the sake of protecting your boss's political vision, you must lead the groups in the direction that your boss would most support. Remember, if you do not lead them, they will lead you, and in the end, they will get what they want and you will not. This happened to me.

I was working on a piece of legislation to increase protections for whistleblowers who work for the federal government. I brought together the various groups, including the White House, other congressional staffers, and outside groups who were all interested in the goal of increasing these protections. But each of these groups had their own vision of what these protections should look like. We were working off drafted legislation that my boss had introduced, so the responsibility of leading the coalition fell to me. But because I was a new staffer without well-developed coalition-management skills, instead of leading the coalition, the coalition led me. The result was that nothing got done. All of the various groups fought with me and with each other so much that we ultimately were unable to do anything.

This was an important lesson for me. I lost control of the process and ended up getting nothing when I might have achieved something of a compromise had I been better able to manage the various groups. To be effective at policy coalition management, and to ensure that you end up getting what you want, you not only need to take charge, you need to have a clear vision with clear goals. If you don't, you will get rolled.[12]

Calm

I will never forget being told once by my first boss, before I was about to give a speech, that the most important thing he got paid for was to be calm. He held a post of high importance in the governor's cabinet that required a tremendous amount of specialized, technical skill, and I would not have thought that it was his calm that the governor valued most.

He reminded me that since we were working in a political environment, our actions were constantly scrutinized and weighed by the public, and they would judge us harshly not because they secretly hoped we would fail, but because they wanted to feel that they were right to have voted for our boss. When you are in public, you need to remember that they expect you to be calm not just in a crisis, but at all times.

One of the reasons President George W. Bush chose Colin Powell to be his secretary of state was because Powell's public persona and style conveyed gravitas and calm. As chairman of the Joint Chiefs of Staff, Powell had helped lead the country through a successful war, and along the way, he developed a reputation for being extraordinarily competent under highly stressful conditions. His legendary calm was on full display as the events of September 11, 2001, unfolded.

Powell was on an overseas mission in a meeting when an assistant whispered in his ear that the Twin Towers were under terrorist attack. Everyone in the room later remarked on how calmly Powell took this news. Without any show of distress, he continued to facilitate the meeting and calmly brought it to a close, without giving any indication of what he had just been told. When the meeting ended, he waited until he boarded his plane for the return flight home to go into crisis mode.

As a highly experienced government staffer, Powell knew that he and the Bush administration would be judged by how he conducted himself. He also knew that his foreign hosts also knew that the Towers were attacked and, though they appeared supportive at the time, were watching him closely and measuring his reactions. Powell knew that they would judge him and the president on how he conducted himself in the immediate aftermath of the crisis. Instead of falling into crisis mode in front of his hosts, Powell waited until he could do so in private. This is the standard that you must emulate in all of your dealings with the public— complete composure, no matter how serious or minor the occasion.

You need to do whatever you have to do to develop this quality. It is, without a doubt, one of the most valuable qualities the best staffers possess. Even if you have no other quality than this one, it will place you in a category above many of your colleagues and competitors who don't possess it.

Command of the Issues

By now you understand enough to know that an elected official is responsible for a large number of policy issues that he could not possibly attend to without the help of staff. As a staffer, it is your job to stay on top of these issues for him. And the stronger your grasp on the issues in your policy portfolio, the more you will be appreciated. It is crucial that you understand why you should take special care to do so.

First, the pace of your environment will work against you. This is where the hours you spent during slow periods mastering the details of an issue will pay off for you. As the one your boss has designated as his point person on the issues, he will look to you to answer any of his questions quickly. He will need the answer then and there, and you must be able to supply it.

You will find that you will be spending so much of your time responding to the pressing matters of the day that you will not have time to make decisions about whether to support or reject a political issue. This is where your grasp of the underlying principles of a subject is key.

Lord Burghley had a foolproof method for mastering the intimate details of subjects—long hours of reinforcement. As her chief minister, he was involved in every detail of Queen Elizabeth's reign. To achieve the depth of knowledge necessary to be able to advise the queen on literally every policy issue, Burghley spent long hours each day writing, filing, rereading, and rewriting memos on all the policy issues he covered. He said writing out memos on policy issues helped him explore and understand the contours of subjects and that putting his thoughts on paper helped him whenever he had to explain the issue to the queen. I adopted this method as well, and though I have to admit it is very time consuming, this approach assures that details will be at your finger-tips when you need them.

You will find that it's not enough to keep files of policy papers and newspaper articles written by other people. You need to sit down with the issue, unpack it, take notes, and explain it to yourself. So, you should write and maintain a memo library for yourself on the issues the way Lord Burghley did. Granted, maintaining such a memo library is hard work. Burghley could be found sitting at his desk long into the night, working on memos. He spent a number of Christmas Eves at his desk doing just that. But in the end, no one had a better grasp of the issues than he and the rewards he received from the queen for his diligence are too numerous to count. Burghley is the standard. If you want to have a limitless career as a policy staffer, hard, sometimes bone-crushing work, is the price.

Finally, mastering procedure should also be one of your main long-term goals. Another of the most valuable skills any staffer possesses is his understanding of the process by which things get done. It doesn't matter if it's the county council, city hall, or Congress; understanding the process by which things get done is almost as valuable as understanding policy. After all, a staffer will be responsible for a whole range of policy subjects in his career and they can change at any time, but process rarely changes. What makes mastery of process such a challenge is its complexity, which can take years to grasp. While you are in the arena, you should take the time and use the resources at your disposal to deepen your understanding of process. Doing so successfully will help to separate you from the also-rans.

To master procedure, you need to throw yourself into the process of learning how things get done in the institution where you work. If you work for a legislator, that means learning floor procedure, committee procedure, how to move legislation, and how to shape it. You need to devote yourself to learning everything about how to get things done—where to go, who to see, and what to say when you get there.

Political Instinct

Political considerations are such a vital part of giving good advice to an elected official that even the most seasoned staffers sometimes experience moments of doubt about their instincts.

That's why I was so confused one day when my boss, a person with almost forty years of political experience, told me that he thought I had good political instincts. I was still relatively new to politics at that time and was questioning my decision making almost daily. After some reflection, I understood why he thought I had good instincts. I also immediately realized that good political instincts could be taught. I'll get to that in a minute, but first I think I should explain why political instincts are so important.

In politics you sometime have to make decisions quickly, so you must not only understand the issues you are dealing with, you must also understand the political ramifications of your decision making. In politics, there are winners and losers on both sides of any issue. Every decision you make has the potential of making an enemy for you and your boss. Under such charged circumstances, the costs of every decision, even the seemingly most benign, must be weighed carefully before it is made. The ability to quickly and correctly weigh the political consequences of a decision requires instinct, and just as it can be learned, it can be taught.

Obviously, the more experience you have, the better you will be at foreseeing the political consequences of a decision. If you are just starting out and don't yet have a good grasp of the issues in your portfolio, you can still exercise good political judgment if you keep a few key things in mind.

First, your job is not about you—it is about your boss. You are serving him. You are being paid to be his eyes and ears and brain. So when you think about an issue, approach the issue from the standpoint of how it will impact him, his reputation, and what he cares about most—winning reelection. You must remember, where politics is concerned, the right thing to do is often not what *you* think the right thing to do is, but what *your boss* thinks is the right thing to do. And when your boss is thinking about what is right, he is thinking about his future and his reputation.

History is rife with examples of staffers whose own ambitions clouded their decision making, weakened their political instincts, and resulted in them losing their jobs. If you always remember to filter any decision or recommendation you make through the lens of how that decision will impact what is most important to your boss—his reputation and chances for reelection—your political instincts will be on the right track.

Second, avoid making snap judgments as much as possible about issues that have direct impact on your boss. Take a moment to consider an issue before making a decision. Again, this seems like an obvious point. But, when you are under pressure, such as in the cases I described above, you will be tempted not to consider an issue as carefully as you should. Take a minute to step back and think about how a decision will affect your boss—even if the issue seems like a no-brainer. You don't want to suffer the embarrassment of having a recommendation shot down immediately for what later seemed like an obvious reason that should have occurred to you.

Third, know your boss, his politics, his priorities, and his district. I'm not saying you need to do a Vulcan Mind Meld with the guy—though, that would be ideal. I'm just saying that you need to know what the issues were that won your boss the election. What do his constituents care about most? What is the local media saying about your boss and the issues? Find out what your boss's reputation is. How is he viewed in his district? Answering these questions early on will help to sharpen your political instincts and make you a valuable member of the staff.

Fourth, in politics, there are *no* secrets. I repeat: *in politics, there are no secrets!* Courtiers with the best political instincts know this and they know how to use this knowledge to their advantage.

Politics is a social enterprise. People meet and people talk. Benjamin Franklin understood this only too well. He was surrounded by spies when he represented the United States at the French court during the American Revolution. Even his personal assistants were spying on him. But Franklin was no dummy. He understood that there was no way to get around the fact that spies were everywhere. He knew whatever he told anyone would eventually make the rounds at the French court. So, he used spies to his advantage to help spread misinformation.

Like Franklin, if you approach your work as if anything you say or do, no matter how closely guarded, will eventually be known to the public, you will be more careful about what you say, and you will be able to make better assessments about what you hear and see. Those better informed assessments will manifest as better political instincts.

And, lastly, be paranoid. There are people out there watching for that moment when your boss muffs up. You need to be mindful of this and act in a way that always protects your boss. That means being suspicious: questioning what you hear and see and thinking about how every issue will impact him.

If you employ these techniques, you should be able to demonstrate good political instincts even on your first day on the job.

Qualities Good Staffers Must Only Appear to Possess

Devotion

There are some qualities, like devotion for example, that a courtier should demonstrate but never actually possess, because if he practices that quality too faithfully, it can harm his career. I guess you can pretty much say that about anything. Take empathy for example. There is a point when you can be too empathetic, and if you are a manager, being too empathetic could make it hard to make difficult personnel decisions. But in politics, where devotion and a low profile are held in high regard, it can be difficult to know when to pull up on the horse.

Take Harry Hopkins for instance. Roosevelt adored Hopkins because he knew Hopkins was devoted to him. But Hopkins's devotion came at the expense of his health. The work and demands of public life wore him down and quickened his demise. To me, this is the greatest lesson of Hopkins's political life. Unless you suffer from a martyr complex, there is a point where devotion is just not worth what you might gain in return. Devotion, true devotion, to a prince is not a quality any staffer should possess.

You are probably asking yourself, is he telling me to not be devoted after spending so much time in previous chapters telling me how much I should be? I am, but this is not so much a contradiction as it is an expression of the nuance of the art of political survival.

To understand how it is possible to be devoted and not devoted at the same time, consider Castiglione's sprezzatura concept. Sprezzatura and the qualified devotion I described in chapter 2 are two concepts that actually have much in common. Today when scholars think of sprezzatura, they tend to reflect only on the positive aspects of the concept—how elan and elegance of manner are noble and enviable qualities. However, in Castiglione's day, sprezzatura had a slightly sinister aspect. Sprezzatura suggested that one's skills need not necessarily be effortless—they only needed to *appear* effortless. Castiglione was saying that even if you were not very good at something, there was still the possibility that you could look as if you were. It is in this way that sprezzatura is similar to devotion. Like sprezzatura, you can appear to be something without actually being that thing. This is particularly important to those of you just beginning your careers who might think you must be prepared to open a vein every time you come into work to prove your devotion to your boss. You don't need to open a vein—you only need to appear as if you are willing to do so.

Understanding the importance and the destructiveness of something like devotion could take years to fully grasp. You should start struggling with this contraction and what it means to you personally now, rather than later when the stakes might be higher.

Alexander Haig offers a good example of how things can go horribly wrong if you are blindly devoted to your boss. His devotion to Nixon could have led to a prison sentence.

Following Nixon's instructions, Haig ordered wiretaps on his colleagues at the White House because Nixon was worried about spies and leaks in his administration. Haig was in charge of determining whose phone to tap and ensuring that the wiretaps were done. Believe it or not, even in the Nixon White House in the 1970s, this was illegal. Haig escaped prosecution, but because of his role in the affair, he carried around a stigma of immorality throughout the rest of his career.

My own experience with the harm that blind devotion can do occurred during a campaign I helped run early in my career. My boss decided that he wanted to challenge one of the political lions of my state. He wanted to challenge a former governor and one of the most important political figures the state had produced in the past century. As you can imagine, the governor had friends everywhere. I knew my boss was going to lose, and I knew that I would probably pay a political price for helping him. But he had helped me many times in my career, so when he declared for office, I was one of the first to call and volunteer my support.

He lost and he lost big. For a time I was a big loser too. Aligning myself with him cost me a lot of political friends. People I had relationships with stopped taking my phone calls and, for a time, I stopped getting invited to political events. I just suddenly dropped off the map. I was lucky in a way because I was so young that I was able to bounce back—I was able to find a job in another state and restart my career. But others on the campaign weren't so lucky. I should have just had a fund-raiser for him and receded into the background. But I was a kid; I didn't know any better.

Being a team player is an important part of being in politics. I am encouraging you to be a team player, but I also want you to understand that sometimes being a team player can come with a high price. Devotion at all costs is not wise. Five hundred years ago, during the Elizabethan age, blind devotion to a prince could result in you getting your head handed to you—literally. Today, the consequences of blind devotion can result, at worst, in a prison term, and, at least, in a blow to your character or career.

If you want to succeed in politics, you need to always appear devoted, but if you want to survive, you should never actually be devoted. Blind devotion is simply too costly.

The Low Profile

The other quality a staffer must display but not really possess is anonymity. Elected officials do not like to compete with staffers for the spotlight. Remember, they are in the business of politics because they want to be the center of attention. The last thing they want is to have to compete with a person on their payroll. Look at Kissinger and Nixon's relationship.

The president complained often about how Kissinger's rock-star status was diverting attention away from him and his policies. Nixon recognized Kissinger's brilliance as a foreign policy strategist, but he thought he had many gifts in this area as well, and he resented Kissinger for getting credit for everything. Kissinger's gifts and the fact that he worked for a person who put these gifts above any of his bad qualities secured his position on Nixon's staff, but Kissinger's situation is the exception, not the rule.

Consider Richard Holbrooke, whose career suffered considerably from his reputation for seeking the spotlight. Holbrooke's last government post was as special envoy to Pakistan and Afghanistan in the Obama administration. He succeeded in landing this tremendous job, despite suffering wide opposition from people who secretly accused him of being a shameless self-promoter and an egoist. He won the job because the secretary of state lobbied heavily for him and because of support from a network of friends he had developed after decades in public service. But his ego almost cost him the post, and, had he not died of a heart attack while in the job, might have been the reason for his eventual dismissal.

Holbrooke's talent for self-promotion and his textured understanding of the power and influence of the media and its utility for amassing influence in Washington was ultimately the source of his undoing. President Obama did not value staffers who sought out the spotlight the way

Holbrooke did, and it led to Holbrooke becoming marginalized in the White House.

The final straw might have been the sweeping and epically flattering magazine article published in the *New Yorker* that, while accurately written, profiled Holbrooke in grand and majestic terms with little mention of the president. A man of Holbrooke's considerable experience should have known better than to submit to such an article. But his ego got the better of him.[13]

In the eyes of a politician, a low profile and devotion go hand in hand. As a staffer you will be expected to recede into the shadows and to nod approvingly as your best ideas are attributed to your boss. The question then becomes: How do you promote your talents and build your reputation without risking being viewed as competing with your boss?

First, you should use every available opportunity to discreetly advertise your abilities. Interactions with your colleagues or with the public at any event where your boss appears should be seen a chance to advance your career and your image. Remember, if your boss is well prepared and gives a great presentation, you as his staffer will be seen as having played a part in his success.

All you have to do is cement the connections between the good job your boss is doing and your skill as a staffer. If your boss is generous, he will acknowledge your work in public. But if he does not, you can still get some of the credit. Fuss over him before he makes his presentation and check up on him often to inquire whether he needs anything. Interact with him as much as possible so that your connection to him and the role you play is recognized by those in attendance.

Second, remember that impressing your colleagues can be as important as impressing your boss. Harry Hopkins once famously said that if you ever want to get something done in Washington, don't bother going to the guy in charge, focus on his staff instead. This is true in every political town, not just Washington. You should view every time you are in the presence of another staffer as a chance to show how well prepared and professional you are.

You can be anonymous and conspicuous at the same time, if you do it right. When I was a White House intern, as a way to set myself apart from my colleagues, I decided I would research and prepare a directory of all foreign policy staffers working in the administration. The task required me to reach out to every agency, often into individual divisions in agencies, because most agencies were unaware of all the foreign policy staffers who worked for them. I worked late into the evenings, often after leaving my job as a waiter at an area restaurant. I worked weekends and between classes. It took three months to assemble and format it all and it sat unacknowledged on my boss's desk for a week until one day, out of the blue, I was asked to assist my boss at an emergency meeting of White House foreign policy experts.

At one point, one of them stood up to say that it would be great if there was a comprehensive directory of foreign policy experts available that they could use to stay in touch after the meeting. I couldn't believe it! This was the very thing I had been working on in private for the last few months!

Before the meeting ended, I gathered up all my fellow interns and we rushed off copies of the directory. With a few copies in hand, I approached my boss and showed him one. He was surprised and impressed. Before the meeting ended, he announced to the room that someone on his staff had been working on the directory mentioned earlier and if anyone wanted a draft copy, the staffer could be found in the back of the room. Thus, in a single discreet act I was able to distinguish myself in the eyes of my colleagues and impress my boss. I didn't have to be in the spotlight to be recognized. And even if my boss had decided to take all of the credit and decided not to recognize me for my efforts, he and my colleagues would have known what I had done.

If you do good work, there will always be opportunities for your good work to be recognized. You will need to discreetly take charge and seek out opportunities to showcase your abilities wherever they present themselves. But at no time should you ever promote yourself at the expense of your boss. When you are in the public eye, your ideas should always be characterized as his ideas. Your talents should be attributed to his ability to bring out the best of what you have to offer. If you find yourself in the spotlight, pretend not to like it so much.

Two Qualities a Staffer Must Never Appear to Possess

Vanity

Cardinal Thomas Wolsey was a vain man. He was the son of a shoemaker, who with luck, intelligence, and a bone-crushing work ethic rose to become the most powerful man in England when Henry VIII tapped him for the post of chief minister. Wolsey was justifiably proud of his accomplishments and took every opportunity to remind those around him of his success. He ignored the frequent warnings to hold his vanity in check—even when they came from the king himself.

Wolsey surrounded himself with the trappings and symbols of power and often made the mistake of speaking to dukes and other powerful noblemen as if he were their equal. Though his conduct bred wide resentment, his power protected him until he made a grave mistake that cost him the support of the king.[14] His resentful enemies seized on the opportunity to quickly sweep him from power. In the end, his vanity cost him his job, though it might have cost him his life.

Machiavelli instructed in *The Prince* that vanity and ego are a lethal combination in a staffer. Even more importantly for someone like you who is just beginning a career in politics, you need to recognize that in the incestuous world of politics, where word of mouth has as much power as a résumé, a reputation for being vain can bring an immediate end to your career even before it begins. Vanity is dangerous in a staffer because it breeds enemies in a profession where making enemies is a natural occurrence. Showing your colleagues that you are arrogant or a narcissist is hardly the path to making friends and influencing people in a job that is all about people and relationships.

Now, you're probably thinking about all the past and present staffers and ministers who, despite their vanity, rose to greatness. It is true that there are some truly vain staffers who, despite their vanity, became great.

Henry Kissinger was vain. Still, Nixon tolerated his vanity because he was a foreign policy genius. Genius also protected Wolsey for a while. If you study the lives of the great staffers of history, what becomes clear is that though vanity may be tolerated for a time, eventually the vain pay a price.

Let's go back to the Henry Kissinger case for a second. Yes, Kissinger enjoyed a stellar career in the Nixon White House. He was perhaps the most powerful national security advisor the United States has ever known. He went on to a successful stint as secretary of state and won the Nobel Peace Prize. But luck was a major factor in his success. Everyone gets a little luck in life, but Kissinger had a little more than most.

Kissinger was the very definition of paranoia, hyper-competitiveness, and vanity when he worked for Nixon. But Kissinger was lucky; he worked for a man who shared these qualities and, in fact, encouraged them in him. Nixon's desire to have total control over national security and foreign policy meant that he had to neutralize the influence of the defense and state departments. To accomplish this, he needed a right-hand man who could keep a secret, who was always looking anxiously over his shoulder for emerging threats, who was an exceptional internecine warrior, and who possessed an ego large enough to bully constitutional officers. Henry Kissinger was the perfect embodiment of these characteristics. But the same qualities that made him invaluable to Nixon would have branded him too difficult to work with for anyone else. His oversized ego had hurt him professionally before.

In the 1960s, Kissinger joined the presidential campaign of Governor Nelson Rockefeller as foreign policy advisor. When Rockefeller lost, he retained Kissinger by giving him a chance to run an arm of the Rockefeller family foundation. The organization had over five hundred employees and Kissinger was the director. This was his first major leadership post and his abrasive leadership style alienated his subordinates to such a degree that he was eventually removed. Ironically, the qualities that led to his removal at one institution helped him at another.

When he assumed the helm of Nixon's National Security Council, he faced a similar problem, but he was able to succeed because, unlike foundation work, in politics, staffers are used to working with abrasive and difficult bosses. Also, Kissinger was able to assemble only the people he wanted around him, so he chose and retained people who tolerated abuse. But even in this circumstance, Kissinger might not have survived if Nixon hadn't created an environment that was supportive of personalities such as Kissinger's.

As I said, politics is an incestuous world where bad word of mouth can permanently sink your career. Think for a second about the confluence of events that had to fall into place for someone like Kissinger to survive. Not only did he have to be a genius, he had to work for a president for whom foreign policy was his primary interest, and he had to work for perhaps the most psychologically damaged person to ever inhabit the presidency. That's luck.

Unless you are a genius, vanity is a risky personality trait to have as a political staffer. Like Kissinger, you will have to be extraordinarily lucky to be successful. If you're not a genius, there are tons of people who are just as smart as you, and who are willing to work just as hard for less money. Why risk your chance of rising in an environment like this by being vain?

Another form of vanity that should be avoided is vanity in the form of dress. Castiglione thought that there were no hard or fast rules for political dress other than that one should adapt oneself to the custom of the majority. But I believe there are a few key principles that all staffers should follow to convey professionalism and to avoid standing out too much.

Politics is a serious profession, not unlike banking or the law, where flamboyance is not encouraged. If you want to be successful, you want to appear conservative, predictable, and safe. Voters want to be able to trust their elected officials without reservation. Flamboyant dress on a politician sends the signal that he may not be like those he represents. You as an extension of your boss must be mindful of how your boss's constituents see you and how their perceptions of you reflect on your boss. By following these three principles you will be able to convey the professionalism and solemnity constituents expect from their elected officials and those who represent them without sacrificing your personality.

First, avoid dressing better than your boss. He understands the people he represents. He knows how far he can push the envelope and what his constituents will accept. You should let his appearance guide your every interaction with his constituents—including how you dress.

Second, whether you are a man or woman, you should wear clothes that flatter your body. Physical attractiveness is power. In politics, you want to be as attractive as possible without coming off as trying too hard—to avoid conveying the message that you are overcompensating for some secret deficiency you might feel.

If you are tall, wear clothes that emphasize your height. If you are shapely, wear clothes that emphasize your shape, but you should never wear clothes that are too revealing. You want to suggest sex without stating it outright. Even in politics, sex appeal is power, and as a young person you should use all the tools available to you to help you stand apart from those around you.

Lastly, if you are male, you should choose discreet colors, styles, and flourishes that are reminiscent of the priesthood to convey the message of seriousness and solemnity. The colors should be dark and the lines understated. Colorful ties, scarves, and socks should be avoided. Wear conservative but well-shined shoes. If you look as if you might be going to a funeral, you are on the right track. For women my advice is the opposite. Women should were bright colors and well-fitting clothes that accentuate their femininity without overselling it. You don't want to dress too discreetly because politics is still a male-dominated profession and you will need all the help you can get. So don't be afraid to stand out—a little.

French politicians seem to have mastered the style of political fashion. If you need a guide and are a man, run a search on Dominique de Villepin or Nicolas Sarkozy. If you are a woman, look up Christine Lagarde or Ségolène Royal. That should put you on the right track. By following these simple rules, you can appear attractive, confident, and professional without appearing as if you crave being the center of attention.[15]

Open Competitiveness

After more than a decade in politics, I am happy to say I have only one true political enemy. We still work together, but I wouldn't trust him as far as I could throw him. We are enemies because, even though we were on the same team, he let me know early with his actions and words that he saw me as a threat and a competitor. His competitive behavior was regular and personal and he took every opportunity to belittle me in front of my boss. Because I had a boss who could see what was going on, I was able to rise despite his efforts. He rose too, but only so far.

Being viewed by your colleagues as a competitor can be almost as hazardous to your career as being viewed by your boss that way. When Lyndon Johnson was a congressional staffer, he had a competition of personalities with L. E. Jones, one of the two men who worked for him. Johnson was in charge of the office, but L. E., who thought a great deal of his own abilities, would not submit totally to Johnson's will.

Even at the start of his career, Johnson's ego compelled him to dominate everyone around him. Those who accepted his dominance got along with him. But if you were like L. E. Jones, not getting along with Johnson could be an embarrassing and humbling experience. L. E. was a fussy, abrasive, and fiercely ambitious staffer. Despite the fact that Johnson was his boss, his strong personality made it difficult for him to accept Johnson's leadership. Johnson recognized L. E.'s competitive spirit and resigned himself to finding a way to break him. Johnson had a brilliant ability to locate and exploit a person's weakness. He used this ability so effectively that later in his career it would get its own name: *The Johnson Treatment*. Recognizing that L. E. was a neat, "no hair out of place" sort of guy, he found a strategy that established without a doubt from that day forward who was the boss in the relationship. Johnson decided that every time he had to review correspondence with L. E. he would insist that the meeting take place while he sat on the toilet. Johnson would call L. E. into the bathroom, and to ensure that L. E. heard every word clearly, Johnson would make him stand over him in the doorway as he relieved himself. Johnson—game, set, and match.

Vanity and competitiveness are equally dangerous in that they can portray you in the eyes of your colleagues as a threat. Here was another character flaw that Kissinger possessed in abundance. Kissinger was competitive to the point of being dangerous. The last thing you wanted to do if you worked for Kissinger was compete with him. It is no coincidence that the only staffer to work for Kissinger and advance was Alexander Haig. Everyone else was driven away by the unreasonable demands Kissinger placed on them or because he successfully marginalized them. Haig survived and excelled because Kissinger never saw him as an intellectual threat. If he had been, he would never have been hired.

I'm not saying don't be competitive. What I'm saying is don't advertise it. When your colleagues look at you, they should only see a team player. You want to be seen as the kind of person who is always looking out for your colleague's back and someone who can be relied on for help when help is needed. If they see you as a competitor, they will see you as a threat, and everything you do will be suspect.

7 | ON THE MEANS OF ASCENT

*The choice of servants is of no little impor-
tance to a prince, and they are good or
not according to the discrimination of the
prince.*

—Machiavelli

*I knew something important was about
to happen from the smell of alcohol on his
breath. It suddenly occurred to me that I
had worked for Councilman Rogers for
two years and I had never seen him have a
drink. I knew he drank occasionally, but I
had never actually witnessed him doing so.
I was working late and he called me into
his office. We usually sat while we spoke,
but this time he stood, so I stood. His back
was to the window, so I could see that it
was pitch-black outside. I wondered if I
might miss the last bus home.*

"You've been working for Mike for two years now, do you think he is a good policy director?" he asked.

"I think he's fine," I said.

"No he's not," he quickly replied.

I was a little shocked. Up to that moment, I had never heard the councilman say a negative word about anyone, let alone a member of his own staff. Besides, Mike had been with the councilman since day one. Sure, he was not the best Policy Director (PD), but no one knew more about policy.

"It's time to make a change," he said. Now I needed a drink, I thought.

He continued. "He's not really a good manager, is he? He just sits back there in that little hole of his in the corner, typing away. He doesn't manage the staff. I need someone who will take charge and lead the staff. I asked Scott to come back to be the PD."

Where will Mike go? I asked.

"He'll stay here. I'll make him a senior policy advisor or something and he will continue sitting in that hole of his, doing what he does best 'til he retires next year. But Scott will replace him as PD."

Wow. That is cold-blooded, I thought. "He's been doing this for almost thirty years," I said.

"But it's not working out so I'm bringing back Scott to do the job that Mike won't do. Why don't you take off. Do me a favor and don't say anything about this 'til I announce it. Close the door on the way out—I have to make a call."

Mike had worked for the Boston City Council for twenty-eight years. I remember when I interviewed to be one of his legislative assistants, I was surprised to hear that he had worked in government longer than I had been alive. He had been a legislative director for a string of council members I had never heard of. I was impressed that he had so much experience and surprised that someone with so many years behind him would still be just a PD to a newly elected councilman. I assumed it was because he loved his job. He looked like a cross between Danny Devito and SpongeBob, and he was funny—I mean really funny. He told me stories about his kids and we laughed for most of the interview. The subject of my job duties never came up.

"The Choice of Servants Is of No Little Importance to a Prince, and They Are Good or Not According to the Discrimination of the Prince."

If Machiavelli were writing *The Prince* today, just as he would have to say more about the personality of modern-day princes to capture the essence of what drives them to run for office, he would also have to devote more of his book to the subject of the people who work for them. He does not say much about the nature of courtiers, but what he does say is spot-on.

Machiavelli is correct in his judgment that a courtier is good or not good based on the judgment of the prince he serves. After all, the prince is looking for the best people he can find to work for him. It doesn't matter if a staffer thinks of himself as the best policy director in the world if his boss disagrees. The courtier's perception of his value to the prince could be clouded by any number of things. In Mike Cannon's case, I can tell you he thought he was a good policy director. Being one of his employees, I knew otherwise.

Mike never rose above policy director in almost thirty years despite possessing other valuable talents, including being a solid advisor, a better-than-average speech writer, and a genuinely likeable person, because he was a wonk struggling to be a mechanic in a job that required a person be a little bit of both.

Through sheer willpower Mike had managed to survive twenty-eight years in Boston City government as a mediocre policy director when he might have had a stellar career in some other profession. The problem was he didn't see that he was a wonk trying to be a mechanic.

Politics is filled with people like Mike Cannon—people who are drawn into the field without knowing for sure whether they are suited for the profession. In previous chapters, I have discussed the different aspects of life for a staffer in politics. In this chapter I will explain the personality types necessary to be successful in the basic types of jobs that exist in politics.

The morning after Councilman Rogers and I spoke, I arrived at the office hoping for a few minutes alone with Mike. He was often the first person to arrive and I expected to find him in his corner typing away as usual. Instead I found his desk empty, cleared of the familiar stack of papers and books that had served as his fortress against the world for the two years I'd known him—and maybe the twenty-five years before that. On the edge of the desk were three hand-written notes for each of the members of the staff. I picked up the one addressed to me.

It said he had decided to take early retirement and that he had enjoyed working with me. He wished me well and said that he wouldn't be a stranger, so I shouldn't. He said something about wanting to get in under the wire before the new statutory retirement rules for staffers kicked in, but I knew the truth. In the end, instead of suffering through the humiliation of a demotion, he left government entirely. When we finally reconnected a few months later, I was happy to hear that he had taken a job as a government strategist for an education nonprofit and was doing quite well. It was a wonk job.

Mike was unsuccessful in government because he failed to recognize that wonks and mechanics have different personalities and work in different ways. Those differences make them well suited for some political jobs and poorly suited for others. Wonks can have mechanic tendencies and the other way around, but most people in politics are predominately one or the other. Depending on the job you take, the type of personality you have will impact your chances for success. You want to choose a political job that meshes well with your personality to avoid becoming frustrated.

Mechanics are "people" people. They have a talent for quickly getting to the heart of a matter rather than lingering lovingly in the details the way a wonk might, and they often have finely tuned social and verbal skills that enable them to get along well with others.

Wonks enjoy being around people but would prefer not having to deal with them too much. They are comfortable with detail and are more accommodating and tolerant of informational nuance than mechanics—they enjoy looking at an issue from many sides. They are often articulate but may lack the sophisticated social skills of mechanics.

Mechanics tend to excel at jobs that require the organization and management of relationships, while wonks excel at jobs that require the management of information. A mechanic would shrivel up and die if left alone too long, while a wonk would appreciate the peace.

Wonks working in jobs that require the skills of mechanics are not performing at the height of their powers because they are not perfectly suited for the positions they hold. The converse is also true. If you are not a people-person, you should avoid mechanic jobs—they will just be too demanding. Interestingly, it is possible to be a wonk and do quite well in the job of a mechanic—and vice versa.

But, though they may become good at the job, they will never be extraordinary. They won't be the people you see on television on the Sunday morning talk shows and they will not be the people you see standing next to the most powerful politicians in the world.

It's also important to note that within these two categories there are only about a couple dozen unique jobs in politics. It doesn't matter where you work. Being a press secretary for a Miami city councilwoman is basically the same as being a press secretary to the president of the United States. Of course the scale is different, and some of the tools may be more sophisticated at the White House, but the purpose of the job and the temperament of the person performing it are basically the same.

Let's take an up-close look at some key temperaments of political jobs and how they work. Your ability to match your core personality traits to the work will determine whether you will be merely good at your job or great.

Mechanics must be outgoing people. Consider the mechanic job of press secretary. The purpose of a press secretary is to manage the prince's media relations. She is responsible for getting the prince's name in print and keeping it there in the best light possible. And, if the prince is being attacked in the press, it is the press secretary's job to defend him. To do this, the press secretary must have the kind of personality that enjoys cultivating existing relationships and building new ones. He or she has to be direct— if not a little confrontational—and he or she has to have strong personalities that do not shrink from conflict. If the press secretary doesn't possess these traits, he or she will be of little use to the prince.

I have a friend who left her job as a television reporter because she hated the backslapping and aggressive socializing that was such an important part of investigating and reporting the news. She thought if she went into politics she could tone things down some. She lasted for about three years before she had to move on. She had a quiet personality and it took a lot out of her to be the outgoing person that was necessary to build up publicity around her boss—who was just starting out in national politics and was working hard to get noticed. When her boss decided he wanted to launch an effort to build a national name for himself, he replaced her with someone who was better suited to the work.

Wonk jobs, like policy advisor, require a different personality type. Policy advisors are expected to be issue experts. That means they have to dig into the material with both hands and build a solid understanding of the issue. This is simply not possible without putting in the time and studying. To do this, you need to sit alone quietly for as long as it takes to absorb the material. If it takes a day or a week or a month, so be it. Your job as policy advisor is to be able to supply answers when called upon to do so. Wonks have an ability to do this in a way that does not come easily for mechanics. And it is the reason mechanics should avoid wonk jobs.

If you are in school thinking about a career in politics or if you are currently working in politics and cannot figure out why you've hit a brick wall professionally or why you don't like your work, I suggest you reflect on whether you're in the right job.

Below is a table that illustrates where the basic jobs of politics match up with personality types. You can see that the temperament and basic skills necessary to be a press secretary match those of being a chief of staff or a fund-raiser or a community organizer. That is because each of those jobs requires strong social skills and an outgoing personality. On the other hand, the wonk categories include researcher and speech writer. Social skills are not as important in these jobs. Instead, it is more vital to possess the ability to focus intently on one cerebral task for long periods and to be comfortable with the solitude that it requires.

In some cases, jobs call for a person to possess qualities and skills from both categories. Campaign manager is such a job. These hybrid types of jobs depend on the person being comfortable with detail and assimilating information, while at the same time being able to manage personalities. This is a difficult combination and most people are not good at juggling the two.

Take a moment to reflect on your personality and your interests and see where the job you would like to do fits in the two categories. If you choose a job that matches your interests as well as your personality, your will have an easier time in politics. And, if you choose to stay in politics, chances are you won't be looking up twenty years from now wondering if you are eligible for early retirement.

Means of Ascent

WONK POLITICAL JOBS	HYBRID POLITICAL JOBS	MECHANIC POLITICAL JOBS
Constituent Mail Correspondent	Campaign Manager	Press Secretary
Legislative Advisor	Legislative/Policy Director	Chief of Staff
Committee Staffer	Staff Director	Administrator
Campaign Strategist		Campaign Organizer/ Coordinator
Policy Advisor		Fund-raiser
Speech Writer		Community Liaison/ Organizer
Researcher		Scheduler

8 | ON FRIENDS, MENTORS, AND BROTHERS-IN-ARMS

He who is well armed has good friends.
—Machiavelli

The Old Girls Network

Madeline Albright had a problem. She wanted to be secretary of state. But that wasn't the problem. The problem was that she wanted to be the first female one.

She was qualified. She was after all the current US ambassador to the UN; she had served on the National Security Council during the Carter administration; and she had been a foreign affairs advisor to a presidential and a vice presidential candidate. Despite all of this, her chances weren't good.

The competition was fierce. The short list included Richard Holbrooke, a perennial candidate for the post who was coming off one of the greatest foreign affairs victories in US history when he negotiated the Dayton Accords and brought to an end the bloody war in Bosnia; former senator George Mitchell, a giant of the foreign affairs establishment who himself could count among his greatest accomplishments a successful peace agreement in Northern Ireland; and Strobe Talbott, the current deputy secretary of state and longtime friend of the president.

Under the circumstances, anyone in Albright's shoes would have been nervous, but Albright was especially so because it was the 1990s and her gender put her at a supreme disadvantage. Her finely tuned political instincts told her that she needed to turn the perceived liability of her gender into an asset, but she didn't know how.

You can't just roll up and apply for the job of secretary of state. It has to be done discreetly and in a way that leaves no fingerprints.

Albright needed a hook to help bump her up to the head of the line. Her opportunity presented itself buried deep in a Washington Post *article about the proposed candidates, where, when asked about Albright's chances, a secret White House source is reported to have said she placed squarely among the second-tier candidates. That was all the opening Albright needed!*

Holbrooke, Talbott, and Mitchell had spent a lifetime cultivating their contacts in the tightly knit and insulated "old-boys network" that comprised the American foreign policy establishment. Being a woman in the 1980s and '90s meant that was a world largely closed to Albright. So she did the next best thing—she created an "old-girls network" of her own, composed of the powerful female friends she had collected over the years. When the Post *article appeared, she called the gals together and they sprang into action.*

Senator Barbara Mikulski, who Albright knew from Capitol Hill, and former Democratic vice presidential candidate Geraldine Ferraro, who Albright advised during Ferraro's campaign, called the president and Vice President Gore to ask why it was that a woman of Albright's qualifications would be relegated to the second tier of anything. Barbara Kennelly, another congressional friend and the fourth-ranking member of the House of Representatives as well as vice chairman of the Democratic Caucus, called to ask why, after women worked so hard to get the president reelected, would he not take Albright's candidacy seriously.

Dust was being kicked up all over Washington. Phones ringing, letters slipped under doors, words discreetly exchanged in passing at the Occidental. The old-girls were not about to give up without a fight—not this time, when one of their own was so close. This went on for days. Even First Lady Hillary Rodham Clinton got involved.

When the dust settled, the victor emerged wearing a smart dark-blue wool pantsuit and gold button earrings.

Holbrooke, Talbott, and Mitchell would have to wait a little longer for their chance. On January 23, 1997, Madeline Korbel Albright stood in the Oval Office flanked by the president and vice president before a phalanx of flashing bulbs to accept the oath to be the sixty-fourth US secretary of state with members of the "old-girls network" smiling in the background.[16]

"He Who Is Well Armed Has Good Friends."

Friendship is another area where Machiavelli and Castiglione have slightly opposing views. To Machiavelli's mind, friendship was no different than a hammer or any other tool. Castiglione is sympathetic to Machiavelli's thinking on this, but he allows for friendship to be something more.

In *The Prince*, Machiavelli doesn't speak of the kind of friendship you might ordinarily think of when you think about your relationships where you want nothing more from the other person than to hang out and enjoy each other's company. Machiavelli's vision of friendship is based on self-interest alone. Although he does accept that friendship sometimes requires sacrifice, his sense of sacrifice is borne out as a debt of mutual responsibility, not selflessness. He thought friendships were bound, at the core, by a bond of obligation, where you made friends for protection or to serve a pragmatic purpose, like when farmers work together to bring in the harvest, for example. He must have had friends who he regarded selflessly, but those types of friendships are not the subject of *The Prince*. In *The Prince*, he is speaking about political friendships, which are not the same.

Machiavelli would understand completely the logic of Albright's "old-girls network." If it hadn't already existed, he might have recommended that she create it. To Machiavelli, Albright's network served what he believed to be the main purpose of friendship in politics—to work collectively toward a common goal.

Castiglione's vision of political friendship is a bit more generous. Though he acknowledges that true, selfless friendships are difficult to achieve in politics, unlike Machiavelli, he accepts that they are possible. Interestingly though, he qualifies his belief with the comment that, because of the nature of politics, these types of friendships should not be encouraged. I will say more about this later.[17]

Though Castiglione believes that only in rare cases are true friendships at court possible, he would understand the logic and utility of Albright's network. Not only would Castiglione approve greatly of the old girls getting together from time to time to have a beer, he would say that Albright's network satisfied three of his major requirements for successful and efficacious political friendships: the ladies were of a similar professional stature, of the same mind politically, and the relationships demonstrated each member's interest in surrounding herself only with people whose friendship reflected well on her.

By encouraging his reader to surround himself only with people who were professional and well regarded, he was trying to prevent him from forming embarrassing associations that could potentially ruin him down the line. Friendships, like who you work for, can color people's perceptions of who you are and can impact your career. He was telling his reader that if he wanted to be taken seriously he needed to establish friendships among people who had reputations for being the same way. Albright's clique of powerful women was just that sort of arrangement.

I don't doubt that the members of Albright's group felt genuine affection for one another. And this affection probably extended beyond merely getting together to talk and commiserate about common problems they faced as women. But don't lose sight of the reason the group was formed in the first place—to achieve a political alliance. The group was formed out of frustration with a system that excluded women from the inner circle. This made it less about friendship and more about politics. By joining the old-girls network, each member recognized that her membership came with an obligation.

You can make friends in politics, but the friends are not just about companionship, they come with obligations of the sort that Albright exercised when she saw her opportunity to be the first female secretary of state. The old girls may consider themselves best buds, but by design, the purpose of the group fit both Machiavelli's and Castiglione's standards for political friendship where political expediency is the goal. The ladies were friends, they exchanged presents during the holidays, and they got together for drinks on birthdays, but, at its core, their friendship was based on political pragmatism. In the end, they were linked together with a kind of pact of obligation to one another. In such political alliances, if any member loses his capacity to bring benefits to the group, he loses his claim to full membership. They might remain friends, and he might still be invited to happy hours, but he is no longer a full card-carrying member of the alliance, because in politics, friendship comes with obligations that you must be equipped to meet.

Now, that doesn't mean that as a member of the group you have to give in and do whatever another member of the group asks of you. But be advised, the expectation will be there.

You Gotta Make Nice

Albright's successful use of her network to win the post of secretary of state illustrates how personal relationships help to fuel the machinery of politics. In politics, friendships help to grease the gears and stoke the engine. Without them, the system would literally come to a halt. Politics is about people. It's about serving people and it's about helping people serve themselves. At their core, all friendships formed in politics have strings attached.

Political friendships serve four important purposes to a staffer: they can help you find a job if you lose one; they can help you stay informed; they can help you save time; and they can help you get things done. Politics and political institutions are too complicated for you to try to do things on your own. You will need political friends to succeed.

I always tell interns that the single most important thing they should accomplish as interns, even more important than learning how the place works, is to make friends with their fellow interns. The friendships you form as an intern in politics can impact your professional life throughout your entire career.

Everyone knows you have to make friends in the workplace. But what I'm trying to tell you is, you literally cannot survive and function in politics without friends. There are jobs where they say it's not what you know, it's who you know. Politics is one of them.

For example, let's focus for a second on the process of finding a job. First, because the entry level jobs in politics are so easy to fill, they don't stay open for long. For someone like yourself, just out of college, the jobs you would be qualified for can be done probably just as well by just about anyone, so the competition will be intense. Second, at your level, jobs are not necessarily advertised— also because they can be filled pretty easily. As soon as an opening comes available, names of potential candidates start popping up. That's why having friends is so crucial. A good network of friends will enable you to know when a job opens up so you can get your name in the mix immediately. You'd be surprised how many people don't get this! I'm going to go out on a limb here and say this because, after more than a decade, I haven't seen anything yet to disabuse me of the belief: you will never get a job in politics without the help of a friend.

Then, once you get the job, you need friendships to help you keep it. In politics, information is power and the best staffers start immediately building the information networks necessary to access the information they will need.

I can remember that when I first started attending committee hearings with my boss, I noticed the same three young staffers huddled in one corner whispering during the beginning of every hearing. I assumed they were strategizing, but later I discovered that they were just trying to figure out what was going on. They were new like I was and they probably felt as clueless as I did. That image of these clueless guys huddled in a tight knot in a corner taught me a valuable lesson. Nothing useful comes from conferring with the uninformed. I decided at that moment that I would focus my energy on identifying and befriending those staffers on the committee who were truly informed. The network of friendships I developed that year is a network that I continue to draw on for information even though my boss no longer sits on that committee.

Another way friends help is when you need to retrieve the answer to a question fast. One member of congress I know insists that everyone who accepts a job on his staff remain for at least three years. One of the reasons for this is that it takes time to learn to work the knobs and switches of politics. When you need an answer quick, you don't want to waste time locating an expert and then waste more time trying to figure out how to get out of them the answer you need. You want someone to help you cut through the bull and get to the heart of the matter.

Friendships can also provide protection. Before Armand Jean du Plessis became the great Cardinal Richelieu and chief minister to King Louis XIII of France, he had to live through a succession of French leaders that included not only Louis XIII but also his mother Marie de Medici, Concino Concini, her favorite minister, and the Duc de Luynes, who replaced Concini. When Richelieu finally rose to power, he filled court appointments with friends and family to act as an early warning system to alert him to emerging problems that could threaten his hold on power. The friendships you form can serve a similar purpose by helping you stay informed about your surroundings and providing an early warning of difficulties ahead.

Additionally, friendships not only help you get the information, they help you get the truth. Just like those clueless staffers I described huddled in the corner of the committee hearing room trying to figure out amongst themselves what was going on, there are thousands of staffers just like them at any given time on phones across this country blindly scrambling to extract answers from other people who themselves don't have a clue. Don't end up being one of them. You need to devote time and energy to connecting with the people with the answers. In the long run, friendships with them will help you save time and get things done.

So, make friends! Form a club or join one and become leader the way that President Lyndon Johnson did when he was a congressional staffer. Go to a happy hour, and if there aren't any happy hours, organize one. Do whatever you have to do to build up your contacts. You will not survive in politics without them. Don't distract yourself with thoughts about whether they think you have an ulterior motive. Of course it helps if you genuinely like them or have something in common with them—but don't let the lack of chemistry stop you. The bottom line is that you must build professional friendships if you hope to survive in politics.

Friends, Mentors, and Brothers-In-Arms

I can't recall the exact date the rose-colored glasses were lifted from my eyes politically, but I remember the moment. It was when I realized that a friend and mentor had betrayed our friendship for political gain. I thought he had invited me to dinner to offer advice about the city council race I was working on, when he was actually there to gather intelligence about the campaign. The significance of the questions he was asking and the reason for his insistence on seeing our stockpile of yard signs and campaign literature didn't occur to me until we were saying our good-byes after dinner. As I watched his car pull out of the parking lot, I felt stupid, embarrassed, a little scared, and deeply sad all at once. Campaign veterans reading this will not be surprised by this story. Either they or someone they know has been burned by a friend in politics. Friendships in politics, even good friendships, aren't like the ones you grew up knowing.

There are four types of friendships in politics: acquaintanceships, political friendships, brothers-in-arms, and mentorships. Each of them is valuable for different reasons, and you should make an effort to establish at least one friendship in each category.

Acquaintances are people you say hi to in the hall or who you run into occasionally at parties. They don't really know you and you don't really know them. But these types of friendships are valuable and you should try to form them. As I have said, politics is about information. By diligently maintaining acquaintances, you help to improve your access to information. One day you may be at an event where you don't know anyone, wondering what's going on, and you will see someone who you've only ever said hi to in passing in the hall. It's situations like these where being nice to everyone pays off. If that acquaintance can fill you in on what's happening, the relationship is worth all the smiles and hellos you've exchanged in passing.

Political friends are people you share a professional history with or those with whom you've formed an alliance. Maybe you worked on a project together once. They usually owe you a favor or maybe it's you who owes them one. They will almost always take your call because they know you would do the same for them. These relationships will be the backbone of your network. You need to do whatever you can to cultivate and maintain these friendships. When they phone—take the call. Return their emails, and if they ask for a favor—do it or explain to them why you can't.

Brothers-in-arms are people you've been in the trenches with. These friends you know best and they are the most likely to put their necks on the line for you. You will have formed a personal bond with them by working long hours together on a project, like a political campaign. They are the ones you call when you need to have a drink. But, remember, this is politics and these friendships are no different than any other type of political friendship in that they come with obligations. Because of this, as long as you both remain in the same business you will never make the transition to a genuinely selfless friendship, because one of the main reasons you remain friends is because you see the professional value in doing so. Nonetheless, these people are the closest you'll come to real friends in politics.

You can trust brothers-in-arms more than most because you've seen each other at your best and worst, you've spent time together during nonwork activities, and you've cried on each other's shoulders at some point. These are the people you blow off steam with. You can be yourself with them and you can be honest—to a point.

This brings me back to the point I introduced earlier where Castiglione says that true friendships are possible, but they should not be encouraged. When you find the section in his book where he says this, you see that he doesn't elaborate a great deal, but I think the reason he makes the distinction is because he wants you to know that you should allow yourself to be totally honest with only a few people in politics.

Earlier I warned you that there are no secrets in politics—this is one of the reasons why I made that point. Sure, you need brothers-in-arms to blow off steam with. Politics is stressful and demanding and you need a friend who you can be real with. But while blowing off steam, people often say things they might regret, such as disparaging things about their bosses or others. Because there are no secrets in politics, you should assume that everything you say may eventually be repeated—that includes private trash-talking to a brother-in-arms.

In politics, information is power, even information gathered over cocktails after work. This is why you must be discreet when discussing sensitive matters in public— even with friends. Discretion is also important because you don't want people to be suspicious of you or have to feel as if they must be careful about what they say around you. If you talk trash about someone to a friend, at some point your friend will begin to wonder what you might be saying about him behind his back. To be safe, you must assume that anything you say and write will be repeated—even to your closest political friends.

I remember in the earliest days of my career sitting on the steps of the State House one quiet night with a friend as he told me how a close friend of his betrayed him and because of it, he had decided to compartmentalize his friendships. The friend had revealed one of his most closely guarded secrets and probably thought that the information would never be repeated. My friend decided that from that day forward, he would have political friends and nonpolitical friends. At the time I didn't think much of his comment, but the statement stuck with me. Now, more than a decade later, I understand what he means.

The last political friendship is the mentor-mentee relationship. Mentors perform a multitude of functions. Not only can they introduce you to the right people and recommend you for a position, if you are diligent and observant, they can provide you with an example of how to be and what to do to succeed. Consider Larry Summers, treasury secretary to President Clinton and key economic advisor to President Obama.

Summers began his political career as a crude, combative, arrogant, and abusive economics advisor to Ronald Reagan. Given how relationship-driven politics is, his career might have ended there had he not crossed paths later with Robert

Rubin, the urbane, calm, and much-liked former CEO of Goldman Sachs and treasury secretary to Bill Clinton. Rubin immediately recognized Summers's brilliance and despite his crudeness, took him under his wing. Rubin saw past his abrasive personality to the bristling intellect underneath. Rubin admired Summers's ability to conceptualize information and to translate that information into practical terms. He described it as something rarely measured to such a degree in any one person. Summers became Rubin's advisor and Rubin became Summers's mentor. As they worked together, Summers learned by watching Rubin closely what he needed to do in order smooth out his rough edges. He was able to soften his persona enough that as his reputation grew in the administration as a brilliant advisor, Rubin was able to help advance his career.[18]

Though all mentors say they choose to become mentors because they want to give back and nurture the next generation, don't be fooled. This relationship is just like any other political relationship—it has strings attached.

Your mentor will only remain your mentor if you appear to be working toward fulfilling your promise. You are joined by a bond of obligation just as in any other political friendship. That obligation requires you, as the mentee, to fulfill your promise as an up-and-coming young staffer with a bright future. Your obligation is to continue rising, or at the very least, to remain in politics in some important way that brings value to your mentor's relationship with you. You do your part and he will give you advice and introduce you to his friends. If don't do your part, he will move on. Had Summers not improved his public persona, it would have been difficult for Rubin to continue supporting him, and as a consequence, Summers might never have risen to the post of treasury secretary.

So, the bottom line is this: true friends are rare in politics. That is, of course, unless you are working with a family member or you can say you actually held your friend's still-beating heart in your hands on some battlefield in Afghanistan. Otherwise, that person with whom you are exchanging witty emails or saving a seat for at the next briefing should always be approached with a degree of caution, professionalism, and the expectation of obligation. You may not be true friends, but for the sake of your own career and your professional reputation, you have to make like you are.

9 | ON THE ART OF INTERNECINE WARFARE

*Read histories and study there the actions
of illustrious men, to see how they have
borne themselves in war, to examine the
causes of their victories and defeat,
so as to avoid the latter and imitate
the former.*

—Machiavelli

Hamilton v. Jefferson

On the front pages of the nation's newspapers and in the corners of dimly lit drawing rooms, Thomas Jefferson and Alexander Hamilton were at war.

They started out as friends and ideological allies in the days when the American colonies were struggling to break free of British rule. But after the Republic was formed and George Washington had been securely established as president, the common purpose of defeating the British that was the foundation of Hamilton and Jefferson's friendship was replaced by open competition.

They were suddenly locked in a struggle over the ideological future of the nation. Hamilton, now treasury secretary, and Jefferson, now secretary of state, had opposing perspectives on what kind of country the United States should be. While Hamilton strove to increase the influence and power of the federal government, Jefferson strove to retain as much authority as possible for states. While Hamilton worked at the Treasury Department to establish the supremacy of the national government and strengthen the financial health of the country, Jefferson worked at the State Department and through Representative James Madison with Congress to directly and indirectly undermine his efforts.

At this point in their careers, Jefferson and Hamilton were highly experienced and skilled courtiers. Jefferson had already been a continental delegate and an ambassador to France—one of the world's most diplomatically challenging courts at the time. Hamilton had been a New York State and constitutional delegate and an assistant to General George Washington during the Revolutionary War. In the early days, their careers occasionally overlapped, and along the way they developed a friendship and keen understanding of each other.

But as members of Washington's cabinet they served at cross purposes and used their understanding of each other to engage in political combat. Jefferson's strategy was to use access to President Washington to launch a frontal assault on Hamilton's character. He sought to undermine his support with the president and persuade Washington that Hamilton's policies were moving the country in the wrong direction. He found a willing ally in James Madison, at the time a well-regarded Virginia member of the US House of Representatives and a man who had once been one of Hamilton's strongest allies. Together, they attacked Hamilton in the papers and in halls of Congress with a carefully orchestrated plan to build public opposition to his policies and to encourage Washington to fire him.

Attacks on Hamilton's policies eventually became personal attacks. Hamilton was not above getting down in the mud himself, and if the occasion called for it, he could be found slinging it with the best of them. One of the reasons we suspect today that Jefferson fathered children with his slave Sally Hemings was because Hamilton helped to spread the rumor more than two hundred years ago in the press. Jefferson returned the favor by helping to spread rumors that Hamilton was part African.

Jefferson was good at using the press and won many of his gossip battles with Hamilton. But on policy, Hamilton often prevailed because he had one thing that Jefferson did not—a close working and intellectual relationship with Washington. Hamilton knew Washington's mind better than anyone and used that knowledge, along with the easy access to the president earned after years of faithful service, to keep Washington in his corner. Jefferson and Washington had a good relationship too, but Jefferson didn't know the president as well as Hamilton did.

We know now that Jefferson would ultimately lose in his attempt to turn Washington and that Hamilton's vision of a strong federal government would prevail. Jefferson lost not because he wasn't a brilliant infighter but because he controlled too few of the key elements of the battlefield. Hamilton had better knowledge of—and access to— Washington; Hamilton's knowledge of Washington gave him a better understanding of what Washington's vision was for the country; and Hamilton's post as treasury secretary gave him an advantage over domestic policy making that Jefferson did not possess as secretary of state.

Each man, as a skilled warrior, knew that personal attacks and attacks on policy alone would not win their war. They knew they would need good access to the decision maker; an ability to make good assessments of the challenges they faced; control of information; allies; and a willingness to be petty at times. Hamilton more often controlled many of these elements and that is why in the end he beat Jefferson.[19]

"Read Histories and Study There the Actions of Illustrious Men to See How They Have Borne Themselves in War."

Revisiting Castiglione and Machiavelli for their insights on the art of war produces mixed results. Castiglione is largely silent on the subject because he wanted to paint a portrait of an idealistic life at court to go along with his idealistic views of what it meant to him to be a courtier. Machiavelli, realist that he was, dedicated an entire chapter to the subject. Of course, he was writing about actually fighting a war, not the office battles this chapter is about, but if you carefully analyze his chapter, you'll find some useful and easily translatable ideas. He makes two important points that can be particularly helpful to you when you engage in your next office battle, or if you want to avoid one.

First, he says memorize the topography and various features of your country so that you will know how best to defend it. If Machiavelli was advising either Jefferson or Hamilton during their battles with each other, he would interpret this advice to mean: take command of and understand fully the policy areas within their portfolios. Policy is the topography of the political battlefield. Machiavelli would say that just as a field commander should know every nook and cranny of the battlefield, policy makers must know every nook and cranny of the policy issue. This is good advice for you as well. Having command of the policy issues within your portfolio will not only make you a better staffer, it will also help you defend your political positions when the time comes.

Second, Machiavelli says, "Never in peacetime stand idle." For you as a staffer, this means to always stay in fighting shape. The moments you have downtime are when you should be striving to deepen your understanding of policies, strengthening your grasp of the political process, and doing all the other things that will make you an effective staffer. Machiavelli would tell his contemporaries to use peacetime to brush up on their swordsmanship; he would tell Jefferson and Hamilton to use the time to build, consolidate, and strengthen their respective portfolios at the State and Treasury Departments; and he would advise you to use the time to fill in the holes in your understanding of important issues.

During Castiglione and Machiavelli's time, most courtiers were also soldiers. The most successful courtiers were adept at fighting on the battlefield as well as at court. Modern-day courtiers may not have to take to the battlefield the way they did in Machiavelli's day, but they still need to be able to defend themselves.

If you're lucky, all your battles will be minor and with people outside of your office. It's a lot easier to cut someone off at the knees if you know you won't have to borrow the stapler from him in the morning. But sometimes, like Hamilton and Jefferson, you may have to fight your own colleagues. Maybe you will have to fight for access to the prince or for limited office resources or for a promotion. Fighting these types of office wars are the most difficult because they require you to fight in a way that ensures your success, while also minimizing damage to your relationships and your career. You will need sophisticated tools to fight these types of wars.

The best office warriors are paranoid or at least hyperobservant; they have good access to the prince or other decision makers; they are able to influence the flow of information; they make good use of their allies; they are able to establish clear-eyed assessments of their environments; they understand the prince and their fellow rivals; and they are capable of being petty when necessary.

It's no coincidence that many of history's greatest courtiers were also excellent internecine warriors. Alexander Hamilton, Donald Rumsfeld, James A. Baker, Henry Kissinger, and Colin Powell were all extraordinary at fighting office battles because they understood what was necessary to be good, and they were willing to do what was necessary to win. I will unpack what it was that specifically made these office warriors successful in turn, but now let's look at the general skills and tools necessary to be a good internecine warrior.

The Weapons of War

Paranoia

Henry Kissinger is among the kings of internecine warriors because he was naturally paranoid and suspicious. He was always worried about people trying to undermine him or his access to President Nixon. As such, he is a good subject for observing the strengths and weaknesses of paranoia as a weapon of war.

Paranoia made Kissinger an effective warrior because it kept him alert and sharp, but sometimes he went too far. Though he assembled an exceptionally able and skilled team around him when he ran the National Security

Council for Nixon, he would not allow his staff to come in personal contact with the president out of fear that they might outshine him in some way. This extended even to his deputy, who Kissinger kept away from Nixon by constantly assigning him busywork. Eventually, the deputy national security advisor quit.

Like Kissinger, you need to "access" your inner paranoia if you want to have a good sense of what's going on around you, but unlike Kissinger, you shouldn't give your paranoia a license to run wild. The purpose of this section is not to encourage you to develop a psychological disorder but to impress upon you two points: First, being a little paranoid is not a bad thing. It helps keep you alert and sharp. Second, sometimes you will have to deal with people who are naturally or even incorrigibly paranoid like Henry Kissinger, who for whatever reason saw everyone as competition and a threat. As sad as it sounds, in politics, people like Kissinger are not as rare as you might hope. It's important for you to see how they operate and what they are capable of.

The Jefferson/Hamilton feud was prolonged and fueled by each man's paranoia. Where Jefferson was paranoid by nature, Hamilton was paranoid by necessity. He was preoccupied with presenting to the world a spotless character and political reputation despite the fact that he was involved in an affair with a married woman that her husband was blackmailing him over. But it was that paranoia that encouraged him to keep one eye out constantly for political attacks.

Being a little paranoid helps keep you alert to what's going on around you, and it will help make you a better warrior if you end up having to fight an office battle. But don't let it go too far. For someone like you who is just starting out, paranoia can do a lot of harm to your career if you develop a reputation for being that way. You can be an effective internecine warrior without having to go overboard like Kissinger. Paranoia is a tool, not a philosophy.

One final word about paranoia. Going back to Castiglione's concept of "sprezzatura," or the art of doing things effortlessly. At the core of the concept is the idea that everyone should always be cognizant of how he or she is perceived by others. The effortlessness Castiglione aspired to was really more about being perceived as having sprezzatura than it was about actually possessing it. Sprezzatura is about image. The first five years of your political career will be about shaping your image. If Castiglione were advising you today, he would say that this is not the time to be developing a reputation for being paranoid. While some might interpret your paranoia as carefulness, others might perceive you as being difficult to work with. That is not the foot you want to start off on as you begin your political career. Though your success as a staffer will depend on you being hypersensitive to your surroundings, you could kill your career if you develop a reputation for being paranoid. So, be selective with whom you share your perceptions and keep as much of your paranoia to yourself as you can.

Information & Clear-Eyed Assessments

Accessing your inner paranoia without a clear and correct assessment of your circumstances can also be harmful to your career. Skilled internecine warriors like Colin Powell and Donald Rumsfeld knew instinctively that good information is a key part of making good assessments. To confirm their suspicions or perceptions about something, they worked to maintain contacts throughout the federal government. This enabled them to gather the most accurate information possible to help them make their assessments.

Because they share areas of overlapping responsibilities, the State Department and the Department of Defense have been waging bureaucratic battles with each other almost since the beginning of the American Republic. For more than two centuries, the State and Defense Departments have fought over money, over who gets to speak for the nation on foreign affairs, and even over seating arrangements at public functions. Things were no different for Colin Powell and Donald Rumsfeld when they ran those two agencies during the second Bush administration. Studying the way Powell and Rumsfeld assembled the weapons of war against each other shows the importance of having good information.

As a former general and a student of history, Colin Powell undoubtedly read *The Prince*, especially the sections on the art of war. As a former naval officer himself, Rumsfeld probably did the same. It's clear from the almost tactical approach they took to assembling information that they understood how clear-eyed assessments of the battlefield depended heavily on having good access to information.

When he accepted the post of secretary of state, Colin Powell tried to get a set of friendly eyes installed at the Defense Department by encouraging Rumsfeld to hire Powell's closest friend Richard Armitage as his deputy. Having Armitage serve in such a high position at the Department of Defense almost assured that Powell would have access to reliable, unfiltered information about that agency. Powell knew that though Armitage might be working for Rumsfeld, his loyalty would secretly be to Powell. But Rumsfeld was no dummy. He was such a skilled infighter that he would have given Machiavelli a run for his money. He refused to hire Armitage. So Powell did the next best thing; he hired Armitage himself and assigned him the task of using his extensive contacts to keep tabs on the Pentagon.

Powell hired Armitage not only to help him gather information but also to help him assess it. This is the same reason Rumsfeld hired Steve Herbits. The Defense Department is the largest agency in the federal government. If it were a company, it would be the largest in the world. Just like running Apple, it's next to impossible to control every detail of a machine that large. But Rumsfeld tried. He knew doing so required him to be intimately informed about the inner workings of the Pentagon—in other words, he needed his own Richard Armitage. He hired Herbits and assigned him the principal task of providing Rumsfeld with assessments of the inner workings of his own agency. Rumsfeld was one of the best internecine warriors because he under-stood the importance of gathering clear-eyed assessments of a situation, and he was willing to do whatever it took to achieve it.[20]

Now, as a low-level staffer, you obviously cannot hire your own Richard Armitage to help you sift intelligence. But what you can do is make friends with somebody whom you can trade ideas with in order to analyze events and information. This is another reason why friends are so important in politics.

Access

As I said above, Kissinger often blocked his staff's access to Nixon and insisted that he be the only one to brief the president on national security matters. He did this because he knew that access was power. In office warfare, access to the prince is essential. Office battles are sometimes petty and about petty things like what the office temperature should be or who gets what shelf in the refrigerator. These battles are not important, but when office battles are about policy—these are the battles you want to win. Often, win-ning these types of battles comes down to a decision maker having the final call. Without access to him, your chances of prevailing are greatly reduced—especially if your oppo-nent has the access that you don't.

All great internecine warriors instinctively understand this. It was the understanding of this principle that moti-vated Clark Clifford to always be the last person President

Truman saw at the end of every day. He knew that if he wanted to influence the president's thinking on any given policy, he had to be the last person the president spoke to on the subject. So, he remained in the office as long as necessary to ensure that when the president began winding down for the night, he was there to see him off to bed. Harry Hopkins went one step further and actually moved into the White House into a room down the hall from the president's. President Carter's national security advisor, Zbigniew Brzenzski, controlled access to the president by tightly controlling the flow of information to him. He insisted that, regardless of who the author was, all memos to the president on foreign affairs should flow through his office. He used this method to chip away at the power and influence of Carter's secretary of state Cyrus Vance.

In the battle between Hamilton and Jefferson, Hamilton ultimately won and Jefferson resigned from government when he finally accepted that Washington was not going to be persuaded by his attacks on Hamilton. The reasons for Jefferson's failure are described throughout this chapter, but chief among them was that Hamilton had better access to Washington. Hamilton had a better relationship with Washington, not only because of their service together during the Revolutionary War but also because Washington grew increasingly suspicious of Jefferson when he discovered that Jefferson was secretly attacking him behind his back.

Jefferson's view of Washington in the last years of his first term was not flattering. True, by then Washington was a greatly diminished version of the person who had led the Continental Army to victory against the British, but Jefferson painted a portrait of Washington to his friends of a man who was dithering and intellectually spent. He told friends that Hamilton was pulling the strings of the administration behind the scenes because Washington was no longer the man he once was. All of this was known to Washington and it did permanent damage to their relationship and to Jefferson's access to him.

Since you will never and should never do battle with someone who is your superior, your battles regarding access will be with your colleagues. And since you are a young staffer, your colleagues will be minor figures on the office food chain. Remember these two bits of advice: If your battle is with a colleague you work with, and the issues are important, make sure that it's only the prince—and no one else—who makes the final decision. Also, make sure you get a chance to air your side with the prince before the decision is made. If your battle is with someone outside of the office, if you can, enlist the help of the most senior person you can in your office. If the issue is important to your boss, you will need to borrow the biggest guns available to you to ensure that you win.

A Little More about Information, Intelligence, and Resources

Kissinger was an excellent warrior, but that doesn't mean he won every battle. Winning is considerably more difficult if you face someone of equal or greater skill. For Kissinger, that person was US Secretary of Defense Melvin Laird. Laird once famously said, "Kissinger is a Machiavellian, but I knew how to beat him at his own game." Laird sharpened his warfighting skills as a long-serving member of Congress. His tenure in Congress taught him the vital importance of controlling the issues that influence policy making and resources. He learned the hard way that if you don't protect what is yours, someone else will swoop down and take it from you.

Laird's instincts told him to keep a close eye on Kissinger. So whenever Kissinger tried to do an end run around Laird, Laird was there to meet him with a smile. Once, during a visit to the Vatican, Kissinger famously tried to exclude Laird from the president's audience with the Pope. Kissinger's desire to control every aspect of foreign policy drove him to cut off access to the president even among his most senior advisors— including the secretary of defense. When Laird got wind of the fact that Kissinger was trying to exclude him from the audience with the Pope, he did what any skilled warfighter would do: he looked for a way to fight back using the resources within his control. In this case, it was military aircraft.

After his meeting with the Pope, Kissinger was scheduled to take a military helicopter, positioned for him in St. Peter's Square, to an aircraft carrier waiting onshore. Seeing his opportunity, Laird delivered the helicopter himself. When the Pope saw the military helicopter landing in the square, he insisted that Laird come inside to wait for the president, who was expected to arrive soon by car. When Kissinger and the president arrived for their meeting with the Pope, Laird could be seen waiting inside smiling and chomping on a cigar.

I'm going to go out on a limb here and guess that if you are reading this book, you are not the US Secretary of Defense. So you probably don't have a military helicopter at your disposal. But what you do have is a policy portfolio—as a staffer, that is one of your most valuable resources.

If your battle is internal to your office, one way to increase your chances of winning is to do whatever you can to prevent others from invading your turf. All good internecine warriors jealously guard the policy issues within their portfolio. They don't allow others to make decisions about their portfolio for them, and they insist on being in the room when the prince needs to be advised on a policy subject that they are responsible for. The best warriors also grab control of issues that overlap with the portfolios of their opponents whenever possible.

Zbigniew Brzezinski's strategy for running Carter's National Security Council was similar to the Kissinger model—he controlled it with an iron fist and he took control of any issue area that overlapped with his own. Like Nixon, Carter wanted the White House, not the State Department, to be the locus of foreign policy making for the government. Like Kissinger, Brzezinski saw this as an invitation to dominate foreign policy completely. That put him on a direct collision course with Secretary of State

Cyrus Vance. The two of them shared a legendary and bitter rivalry that ultimately resulted in Vance resigning. Brzezinski won most of his battles with Vance, not only because he was a brilliant internecine warrior but because he had no problem being nasty when it was necessary. Vance was too much of a gentleman to get down in the mud with Brzezinski. One of the strategies Brzezinski used to wrestle control over foreign policy making away from Vance was to slowly consume Vance's portfolio until Brzezinski, not Vance, was recognized by world leaders and the American press as the voice of the administration on all foreign affairs matters.[21]

If the battle is internal and about a policy issue that is squarely within your portfolio, and if you aggressively guard your turf, you will probably win most of the time. But if the battle is over a policy issue where there is overlap with another staffer, you will need to think about how important winning is to you and whether the issue is important enough to get worked up about. If the battle is external, and it's about policy, it really comes down to whether your boss wants to get involved, because then it becomes a battle between princes.

Allies

No successful internecine warrior succeeds without the help of allies. Even legendary loners like Cardinal Wolsey and Henry Kissinger, who had few if any allies, could at least count their prince as an ally. Fighting an office war without allies is a mistake. You need allies to bounce ideas off of, to help assess conditions on the ground, to help interpret intelligence, and to share the work load. Jefferson knew this and formed a political partnership with James Madison; Colin Powell knew this and enlisted his old friend Richard Armitage to help him fight Vice President Cheney and Donald Rumsfeld; and James A. Baker, chief of staff to Ronald Reagan, mobilized a famous troika of allies during the Reagan administration to help neutralize Secretary of State Alexander Haig. Baker's troika consisted of himself, Mike Deaver, and Ed Meese, the president's attorney general. Together they formed a partnership that enabled them to exercise almost complete supremacy over the cabinet.

James Baker was a model courtier. His keen intelligence, diligence, and finely tuned political instincts helped propel him on a long career in government. He served twice as White House chief of staff, and he was US secretary of state and secretary of treasury. Yet his prince, Ronald Reagan, was a courtier's nightmare. Reagan guarded his personal reactions closely, making it difficult to get an accurate read of his emotions or perceptions: this slowed down the process of policy making. Early in his presidency, before the president's disinterest in the details of policy making were widely known, staffers would return from having briefed him with no idea of whether they were understood or if the president had even been listening.

To ensure that he kept a firm hand on policy making despite Reagan's detachment, Baker implemented the troika strategy. Each member of the troika had a specific responsibility: Baker and Meese split domestic and foreign policy issues and Deaver focused on managing Reagan. The troika worked as a team and were a formidable force. When Haig revealed his ambition to wrestle away control over foreign policy from the White House, the troika focused its sights on him.

Haig's abrasive personality, pettiness, and unwillingness to study the president and adapt to his personality made the secretary of state a difficult person for the troika to work with generally, but Haig only became a target for outright removal when it became clear that he wanted to take away some of the troika's power. It wasn't a single event that made Haig a target but a trio of major mistakes.

First, on Reagan's Inauguration Day, Haig handed Meese a memorandum he had written that clearly showed his intention to dominate foreign policy making. The next major mistake happened later that same year when there was an assassination attempt made on the life of the president. While Reagan was being wheeled into the operating room, Haig was at the White House conducting a press conference where he was telling reporters that, since the president was incapacitated and the vice president was out of reach, he was in charge. Not only was Haig constitutionally incorrect, he had made this comment without consulting with the troika. They agreed that when the president returned to the White House,

Haig's access to him would be reduced and the president would no longer meet with the secretary of state without one of them present.

If there was a final straw, it occurred the day Haig wrote and dispatched instructions to a US envoy who was negotiating an agreement between Israel and Lebanon, following Israel's siege of Beirut. Haig drafted the document but was unhappy that the language was taking so long to be approved by the White House. So, without the approval of the president, the National Security Council, or the troika, Haig decided to send the dispatch himself. This was a direct violation of presidential authority and Reagan came within a hair's breadth of firing him. He did not, but it didn't matter. The troika had already begun the search for his replacement. And within a few weeks, Haig was gone.

You may not be able to create a formal arrangement like the troika, but even a young staffer needs allies. If you choose to remain in public service, I guarantee you that an office battle is in your future. When the time comes, you will need help.

Allies, Rivals, and the Prince

I've shown you the dangers of not understanding the prince: Haig was replaced and Jefferson ultimately lost his ideological battle with Hamilton because they did not understand their bosses. I've shown you the importance of knowing your enemies: Kissinger's understanding of his enemies was the reason he worked so hard to neutralize threats before they emerged, and an understanding of the threat that Vice President Cheney and Defense Secretary Rumsfeld posed was one of the reasons that Colin Powell and Richard Armitage formed their partnership at the State Department.

Now let me show you how a good internecine warrior must also have a good understanding of his allies. You wouldn't think that a good understanding of the people who are helping you would be so critical—but it is. Without a good understanding of your allies, you will never know fully how committed they are to your cause and you will never fully know how far you can push them. Don't make the mistake that Treasury Secretary Samuel Chase made when he enlisted allies to help push Secretary of State Edward Seward out of Abraham Lincoln's administration.

Chase tried to have Seward fired by stoking the jealousy his fellow cabinet officials felt about Seward's outsized influence over Lincoln. Chase also helped to create a negative image of Seward in the media by spreading rumors that Seward was a puppet master and that he was pulling the strings behind the scenes and forcing Lincoln to make decisions that were hurting the country. Chase spread the false rumor that Seward's unfair influence over Lincoln was drowning out the more moderate voices of the rest of the cabinet. You'll remember that this was a turbulent time for the country, when every decision had the potential to impact the nation's unity. This helped make Chase's complaints about Seward appear more urgent.

Though his efforts were crafted to appear unselfish, Chase's efforts were motivated by a desire to increase his own influence with Lincoln and to position himself for a run for the presidency at the end of Lincoln's term. But ultimately Chase failed, and his failure weakened his chances of becoming president and damaged his reputation among his colleagues on the cabinet.

In his quest to unseat Seward, Chase did some things right and some wrong. For example, he successfully cultivated negative sentiment about Lincoln in the Senate in order to build the allies he would need in Congress; he organized his fellow cabinet members who were jealous of Seward's close relationship with the president; and he did all he could to burnish his own reputation among the public as an able administrator so as to be seen as a logical alternative to Seward's leadership. But he made two significant mistakes.

First, he didn't know the prince. Not knowing Lincoln as well as he thought, he underestimated Lincoln's understanding of human nature. Second, he did not understand his allies. He did not fully gauge the commitment of the coalition he had built among his allies in the cabinet.

Lincoln understood Chase. He knew Chase was jealous of Seward and that Chase was criticizing him and his decisions behind his back. He also knew Chase was spreading rumors about the lack of cohesion in the cabinet. Lincoln used his keen understanding of human nature, and of Chase, to turn the whole affair against him. When Chase succeeded in convincing the Senate to pass a bill expressing no confidence in the president's cabinet in order to encourage Lincoln to remove Seward, Lincoln organized a meeting between the cabinet and the senators that appeared to be about giving everyone the chance to air their concerns on the subject, but Lincoln had an ulterior motive. At the meeting, he had each senator express his concerns about the rumors that each was hearing about the operations of the cabinet. Then he invited each cabinet member to confirm or deny whether each of the rumors was true. The object of the meeting was not really to give everyone a chance to express his concerns, but to put Chase on the spot and force him to say to Lincoln's face what he was saying behind his back.

When Lincoln asked each individual cabinet member whether the criticisms about Seward were true, each denied that they were. Each denial made Chase look more and more like a liar. When it came time for Chase to speak, his colleagues expected him to repeat the criticisms he had used in private to attack Seward. Instead, Chase folded. He denied that the rumors were true and insisted that the cabinet was functioning properly.

Two things are clear from this incident: First, Chase did not understand Lincoln well enough to suspect that Lincoln would put him on the spot the way he did. He should have understood Lincoln well enough to know that this was a possibility.

Second, Chase had been a senator and his Senate experience enabled him to calculate correctly the Senate's response to the rumors about Seward, but he didn't correctly gauge how his own cabinet colleagues would respond under pressure. So he was surprised, and ultimately showed up when none of his colleagues in the cabinet spoke up about Seward when they were pressed.[22]

To be a successful warrior, you must understand the prince well enough to predict his behavior and you must fully understand the commitment of your allies. To do anything less can set you up for a fall that could ruin your reputation, your working relationships, or your relationship with the prince.

Ruthlessness

Being nice is such a crucial part of politics that it's easy to lose sight of the fact that there are times when being nice can actually harm your career. Political knife fights are such times. You never want to lose a battle because you didn't defend yourself as well as you could have. If challenged, make it clear from the beginning that you are not to be toyed with. You can do this by squaring up with your opponent and making it clear that if it's a fight he wants—a fight he'll get. That was Alexander Hamilton's approach to political attacks. If you challenged him, he let you know early and often that it was on!

Having a "don't mess with me" attitude is also a good way to avoid a fight. You want people to know that if pushed, you will have no problem ripping their hearts out—seriously. This is especially true if you are a woman or if you are the boss. You want to be nice and easygoing, but remember—in politics, when you get screwed, so does your boss. So make sure people understand from the jump that you are not playing around.

Part of the reason Kissinger and Brzeznski had such rough exteriors was to send a clear message that they were not people to be messed with. I'm not saying you need to be as abrasive as they were, but there must be no doubt that you will cut the throat of anyone who tries to screw you. How you convey that message is up to you, but whatever way you chose to do it, the message must be clear.

Pettiness

As a footnote principle, remember these details: Kissinger and Laird fought over who attended meetings with the president; Hamilton fueled rumors in the press that Thomas Jefferson had fathered a number of children with his slave Sally Hemings; and Alexander Haig fought passionate battles with the troika over seating arrangements on Air Force One. Pettiness is just a part of politics and it occurs at all levels. Sometime soon you will find yourself embroiled in a petty office war with a colleague. My advice to you is to choose your battles carefully. Don't develop a reputation for pettiness that could dampen your chances of getting employment in the future. And don't waste resources and allies on battles that will yield very little in the end.

But also remember, there will be times when pettiness is necessary. A former boss of mine, who was a political legend in my state, once told me, "Never forget who your enemies are in politics." The nature of politics is such that to get things done, you often have to team up with people who have screwed you in the past. But, though you may be working with them today, never forget why that person became your enemy. You may have to soon turn and do battle against them someday, and you need to embrace what you're up against.

EPILOGUE: ON BEING A MODEL COURTIER

"I could not sleep at night with you out of the country."
—President Franklin Delano Roosevelt

So, what's the point of all of this? Why bother with learning how to write and speak like a newspaper reporter when all you really want to do is make policy? Why worry about keeping your warrior skills sharp, and why spend so much time breaking down the term "friendship"? Well, this book has a single aim: to turn you into a political survivor.

To survive as a staffer in politics, you need to be better skilled then your colleagues. Being better skilled will make you a better staffer, and being a better staffer will increase your chances of remaining employed for as long as you want to be. Everyone has bad luck at some point in his or her career—maybe you'll have a bad boss or maybe you'll have an unlucky one. It won't matter because you will now have what you need to fall on your feet regardless of what lies ahead.

Most people know about *The Prince*, but very few people have actually read it. Since you have, you know that Machiavelli didn't write the book for some evil purpose, but for the noble purpose of preparing Italian princes for the difficult task of breaking the grip that foreigners held on Italy. The only way for this to happen, in Machiavelli's mind, was for princes or people who aspired to be princes to have the will and skill to take back the country—by force if necessary. That was the overarching message of the book—but over the centuries that message has been drowned out by other voices wanting to promote the book's less noble and more sensational messages.

Castiglione's book also had a noble message. He wanted to encourage courtiers to aspire to perfection so that they would be perfect advisors to their princes, who he saw as flawed and easily corrupted people. He hoped that if courtiers adhered to the highest moral and professional standards, they would serve as beacons of nobility to their bosses, and that through the good advice of his courtier, a prince would become a better ruler.

Both books also shared the goal of providing their readers with what they needed to reduce the influence of bad luck on their careers. That's why Machiavelli focuses so much on war fighting and why Castiglione encourages the courtier to devote so much energy to perfecting his courtly skills. They were saying: if you are well trained, well-informed, and properly focused, you can limit your chances of defeat.

I hope *The Capitol Hill Playbook* has helped to reinforce the message of those two books for today's courtier by illustrating the enduring value of key skills and qualities to political survival. You have seen what made Clark Clifford such a good communicator; you've witnessed the hazards Alexander Haig faced as he did whatever it took to stay in the good graces of President Richard Nixon; and you've seen how Madeline Albright used her relationships to help her become the first female US secretary of state.

Each of the courtiers profiled in this book was chosen because his or her life presents an excellent example of some aspect of what it takes to be a model courtier. However, it's difficult to say which of them offers the best model, because each was chosen for a different reason.

Clark Clifford is mentioned many times throughout the book and James Baker only a couple of times, but that doesn't mean Clifford is the better model of the two. In fact, of the two men, I would recommend you model your career on Baker's rather than Clifford's because of Clifford's tendency early in his political career of falsely representing the work of others as his own, his mediocre performance as

Lyndon Johnson's secretary of defense, and for the trouble he got himself into late in his career.

Additionally, I might have said more about Robert Moses, who achieved, arguably, the most influential career of all the courtiers featured, but other than being an excellent model for how to accumulate power, Moses had few other qualities worth highlighting.

If I had a favorite, it was probably George Marshall because of the long, selfless, and honorable service he gave to his country.

I knew little of Marshall initially. I decided to research Marshall because I read that Colin Powell had a painting of him hung in the State Department when he was secretary of state. Like Powell, Marshall was a former general who rose to lead the State Department, and I assumed that their common past was the only source of Powell's admiration for the general.

Marshall had a long career, surviving a number of administrations, so I expected my research into his life to reveal a fiercely ambitious man who would stop at nothing to advance his career. What I found instead was a man whose skills and personal integrity put him in a class of courtier that I had not experienced up to that point. I grew to admire Marshall in a way I had not admired any other person I researched. He was the very definition of honor, and yet the arc of his career showed that it was possible to be honorable and still achieve great success. He proved to me that I didn't need the personality of Henry Kissinger to get where I wanted to go. One scene from Marshall's life in particular will forever stand as an ideal illustration of the integrity and honor George Marshall possessed. When I first read about the event, the scene almost brought me to tears.

General George C. Marshall was US Army chief of staff to President Franklin Delano Roosevelt during the start up to America's involvement in World War II. He was a stern man and no one would call him chatty, but he was an extraordinarily honorable man in a business that can sometimes be less than honorable. One of the reasons his name no longer inspires the recognition it once did is because General Dwight D. Eisenhower, the future president, beat him out of a job that, though Marshall was the better man, Eisenhower got because Marshall was too honorable to challenge him for it. When all the dust settled, Eisenhower got the job, became world famous, and rode that wave of fame into the White House.

My heart goes out to Marshall, because I know how much he wanted that job, but his personal code of honor would not permit him to say anything self-serving, even if a chance to make history hung in the balance. How he conducted himself in the run-up to President Roosevelt's decision to award his dream job to someone else should be a lesson to anyone about grace and honor in politics.

I can see him now standing alone in the anteroom suite of the Mena Hotel in Cairo, gazing through the open window at the Great Pyramid off in the distance and mindlessly stroking the face of his watch as President Roosevelt finished a call in the next room. He and the president were in Cairo attending a war conference with Marshal Stalin, the Soviet Premier, and Winston Churchill. He had been summoned by the president to receive his final decision regarding whether he or General Eisenhower would lead "Operation Overlord."

At the age of sixty-three, tall, and with the unmistakable bearing of a man who had spent all of his adult life in uniform, General Marshall had every reason to be optimistic about the president's decision, but as the door opened and the president carefully maneuvered his wheelchair in his direction through the deep Persian carpet that separated them, Marshall could tell from the president's uncharacteristically downcast eyes that the decision had been made and the result was not in his favor. Marshall was about to lose the chance to lead American and European forces in one of the greatest military campaigns in the history of the world—and it would be all of his fault.

Roosevelt had struggled for months to make the decision. On more than one occasion he had secretly decided to grant the post to Marshall. He was, after all, the logical choice. Not only had Marshall developed the military strategy for Operation Overlord, but no other general was more knowledgeable on the subject and no other member of the military commanded the same level of respect. Even Marshall thought he was the best person for the job, but his strict soldier's code of honor forbade him from sharing his thoughts with the president. So, even as the deadline approached for a decision, Roosevelt could not bring himself to make up his mind.

On the one hand, FDR couldn't afford to lose Marshall as his Army chief of staff. He needed him to continue using the respect he inspired among members of Congress to encourage them to maintain their support for the administration's increasingly unpopular military programs. As the United States prepared to take the lead of the most important elements of the war, Roosevelt knew that Marshall's talents and reputation would be needed in Washington more than ever.

On the other hand, he could not bring himself to deny Marshall the chance to lead the most important military operation of the war. The commander of Operation Overlord would undoubtedly be celebrated across the globe as a hero. Marshall had given exemplary service to his country for many decades and he deserved his chance in the sun. So FDR did everything he could to get Marshall to tip his hand and make the choice for him. But Marshall would not.

Marshall desperately wanted the job. Opportunities like these had eluded him throughout much of his long career. Despite being an extraordinarily gifted leader, he watched for years as friends and fellow Virginia Military Institute classmates passed him up the ladder to higher promotion. As he approached retirement age, it was only through the direct help of his mentor General George Pershing that he was able to obtain the rank of brigadier general—the lowest rank in the General Officer Corps. Even his post as chief of staff was awarded to him reluctantly after his friend Harry Hopkins lobbied President Roosevelt vociferously on his behalf. Marshall knew that at his advanced age, this leadership post would probably be his last grasp at history. But commitment to honor, duty, and service to country was the anvil upon which his every action and utterance was forged. He would never presume to advise the president of the United States and commander in chief of US armed forces to select him for the post—even if not speaking up meant the end of his career.

As the story goes, Roosevelt broke the news to Marshall with the words: "I feel I could not sleep at night with you out of the country." As Marshall listened to the president, he reached for a pad of hotel stationery lying nearby. He started writing the letter "I," scratched it out, and began again: "The immediate appointment of General Eisenhower to command of Operation Overlord has been decided upon." He handed the pad to the president and Roosevelt signed it.

If he could see into the future, Marshall would have known his career was not coming to end at that moment and that, in fact, he would experience even greater triumphs in the years to come. He would be the fiftieth US secretary of state, a winner of the Nobel Peace Prize, the third US secretary of defense, and the father of the Marshall Plan—the US-backed effort to rebuild Europe after World War II.

But on that fateful day in December 1943, as he and President Roosevelt sat alone quietly in a hotel room in Cairo, he could not have known this. He accepted the president's decision with honor and grace. At that moment, Marshall might have believed that history would forget him, but it is precisely because of his commitment to duty, honor, and country above all else that he lives on as one of the greatest public servants this country has ever produced.[23]

NOTES

1. Quotations from the works of Machiavelli and Castiglione are largely taken from public domain sources along with the following titles: *The Book of the Courtier*, translated by Leonard Elkstein Qadyke, published by Dover Publishing, 2003; *The Courtier*, translated by George Bull, published by Penguin Classics, 1967; *The Prince and the Discourses*, with an introduction by Max Lerner, published by Modern Library College Editions, 1950; and *The Prince*, translated by W. K. Marriott, published by Alfred A. Knopf, 1992.

2. Most books about Richard Nixon will touch upon the Watergate scandal and offer insight into the personality of the president, but I want to call your attention to three books that provide particularly candid portraits of Richard Nixon: *Kissinger* by Walter Isaacson, published by Simon & Schuster, 1992; *Nixon: The Rise of An American Politician* by Roger Morris, published by Henry Holt & Co., 1990; and *Nixon & Kissinger: Partners in Power* by Robert Dallek, published by Harper Perennial, 2007. I've found that the most illuminating resources about Nixon are often those that describe in detail his relationship with Henry Kissinger. They came from very different backgrounds, Nixon, the son of a poor California farmer, and Kissinger, the son of European Jews who fled to the United States to escape the Holocaust, but their personalities and

weaknesses were remarkably similar. These books will help you understand why.

3. This vignette, adapted from the work of David Lawday, perfectly captures the relationship between Talleyrand and Napoleon at this point in their careers. Like Nixon and Kissinger, the qualities and personalities of Napoleon and Talleyrand brought out the worst in the other. Despite their moral frailties, Talleyrand and Napoleon's relationship, like Nixon and Kissinger's, helped to shape the world we live in today. For a good description of the dynamics between Talleyrand and Napoleon, I recommend you read *Napoleon's Master* by David Lawday, published by Thomas Dunne Books, 2006; *Talleyrand: Art of Survival* by Jean Orieux, published by Alfred A. Knopf, 1974; *Talleyrand* by Duff Cooper, published by Grove Press, 1932; and *Napoleon and Talleyrand* by Barbara Norman, published by Stein & Day, 1976.

4. For a biography of Colonel House and an understanding of his relationship with President Wilson, I recommend you read *Wilson's Right Hand: The Life of Colonel House* by Godfrey Hodgson, published by Yale University Press, 2006, and *Wilson & Colonel House: A Personality Study* by Alexander George, published by Dover Publications, 1964. A good biographical description of Harry Hopkins and his relationship with President Roosevelt can be found in *Harry Hopkins: Ally of the Poor and Defender of Democracy* by George McJimsey, published by Harvard, 1987, and *Roosevelt and Hopkins: An Intimate History* by Robert Sherwood, published by Enigma Books, 2008.

5. Alexander Haig survived to become Kissinger's deputy simply by outlasting his colleagues. Though he was not an intellectual equal of Kissinger, he did possess qualities that made him well suited for a position on Kissinger's staff: his extraordinary capacity for work, his logistical and administrative skill (both along with attention to detail were skills that Kissinger lacked), and an uncommon ability to suffer emotional abuse. Alexander Haig is a fascinating character, whose career in many ways illustrates the harmful effects of overstaying one's welcome in politics. Haig enters the story here at the beginning of his political career when he has little power and influence. As you can imagine, his personality changes as the years pass and his power grows. For an understanding of what he was like at this period of his life, in addition to the books above about Henry Kissinger, see *Haig: The General's Progress* by Roger Morris, published by Playboy Press, 1982.

6. Madame de Pompadour's vision of the world was not very complicated and she was not very complicated. Those who frequently and enthusiastically applied their lips to her derriere were favored and would receive her help; those who did not risked having her as an enemy. It's surprising how many books have been published about the mistresses of famous French political figures, but there are only a few volumes published about Madame de Pompadour. Of them, I found two to be the most helpful for understanding her: *Madame de Pompadour: Mistress of France* by Christine Pevitt Algrant, published by Grove Press in New York, 2002, and *Madame de Pompadour* by Nancy Mitford, originally published by Random House in 1954.

7. When I began this project, I decided that I would feature only courtiers that had worked for more than one powerful prince in their careers because I discovered early on that the most famous and influential courtiers often worked for more than one person, and also because working for more than one prince, in a way, helped to prove they were skilled and savvy—otherwise, they would not have been asked to return to service. Pompadour and Michael Deaver are among the exceptions I made to that rule. Pompadour, for obvious reasons, could only serve one prince, but Deaver might have served another prince if he was more skilled as a courtier. Deaver was a one-trick pony who performed that one trick very well—and that's how he got into this book. For a description of his relationship with the Reagans, see *Reagan: The Man and his Presidency* by Deborah Hart Stuber, published by Houghton Mifflin Co., 1998; *Ronnie & Nancy* by Bob Cocacello published by Warner Brothers Books, 2004; *The Power Game: How Washington Works*, by Hedrick Smith, published by Random House, 1988 and *President Reagan: The Role of a Lifetime*, by Lou Cannon, published by Simon & Schuster, 1991.

8. In the end, it wasn't the politicians who brought Moses down; it was the ordinary citizens of Manhattan who joined together to stop him from building a colossal highway down the middle of the city. Moses was intensely protective of his public image, so there are few revealing books about him. But that doesn't matter; you only need to read one, *The Powerbroker: Robert Moses and the Fall of New York* by Robert Caro, published by Vantage Books, 1975. It is considered the first and last word on Moses and you will find no more thorough portrait of the man.

9. Phillip II eventually outgrew his insecurities about governing and developed into a powerful and influential leader, but Ruy Gomez did not remain at his side throughout his reign. His departure was tinged with a hint of scandal, details of which can be found in *The Courtier and the King: Ruy Gomez de Silva, Phillip II and the Court of Spain*, by James Boyden, published by University of California Press, 1995. For additional information about how Franklin achieved this great foreign policy success, see *Benjamin Franklin: An American Life* by Walter Isaacson, published by Simon & Schuster, 2003.

10. Lord Burghley was a model courtier who rose from humble beginnings to unparalleled influence in the court of Elizabeth I but who faced political death more than a few times during his long career. To learn more about the man and his life, read *The Great Lord Burghley,* which was originally published by Martin Hume in 1898 but was rereleased in 2010 by Bibliobazaar, and *Burghley: William Cecil at the Court of Elizabeth I* by Stephen Alford, published by Yale University Press, 2011.

11. Marshall was not so much married to his position as he was opposed to Clifford using politics to settle a foreign policy issue. In the end, Clifford won the battle over this matter because Marshall did not want to ruin his relationship with the president by pushing the issue further. Watching Clifford's presentation style is truly an experience, and videos of his various interviews still exist and can be found on YouTube. For more about Clifford's preparation methods or about his relationship with President Truman and their work together, see *Counsel to the President* by Clark Clifford, published by Random House, 1991; *The Wiseman*

of Washington by John Acacia, published by University of Kentucky Press, 2009; and *Friends in High Places: The Rise and Fall of Clark Clifford* by Douglas Frantz and David McKean, published by Little, Brown, 1995.

12. Another major problem I had with the coalition I described here was my lack of negotiation skills. Negotiation is a major component of coalition building and it's a major part of policy making. I had some experience with negotiation that I had gained in my work as a legislative assistant, but I had never negotiated with people with the level of skill described in this section. I would have been a little better prepared had I read the book *Getting to Yes* by Roger Fisher and William Ury, published by Penguin, 2011.

13. During my first encounter with Richard Holbrooke, I could tell I was in the presence of greatness. I have been in the room with Presidents Reagan, Clinton, and Obama—none of them had the effect on me that Holbrooke had. He had been invited to testify at a congressional hearing about US activities in Afghanistan. To this day, I have never seen a more masterful command of a committee hearing room than Richard Holbrooke's performance that day. It was if he was holding court. He was in full command of the issues and spoke in inspiring and majestic terms about our role in Afghanistan. He was articulate, supremely confident, funny, and generally likable. I remember turning to a friend and saying that I wanted to be like him when I grow up. Holbrooke was a man's man, a rock star, a giant. Sadly, I was also invited to a dinner at the State Department that occurred not long before his heart attack. He was a greatly diminished figure. The spark was still evident,

but it was clear that the energy was waning. Surprisingly, there are not a great many books written about him. For an accurate glimpse of what he was like, I recommend George Packer's *New Yorker* article, "The Last Mission," published in September 2009. And for an understanding of the friction between Holbrooke and President Obama, I refer you to *The Obamians: The Struggle Inside the White House to Redefine American Power* by James Mann, published by Penguin Books, 2012.

14. The mistake had to do with Wolsey's inability to win an annulment and a divorce for King Henry VIII so that he could marry his mistress Anne Boleyn. Wolsey's difficulties with this task are well documented, but I recommend you read *The Cardinal and the Secretary* by Neville Williams, published by MacMillan Books, 1976, and *Statesman and Fanatic* by Jasper Godwin Ridley, published by Constable Books, 1982.

15. For you guys out there who need a little extra help I recommend reading *The Suit: A Machiavellian Approach to Men's Style* by Nicholas Antongiavanni, published by Harper Business Press, 2006. He goes a little over the top, but it should help you understand the value of sartorial understatement.

16. Video of Secretary Albright's swearing-in ceremony can still be found on the web. From the look in everyone's eyes, this was clearly an extraordinary occasion. Many books have been written about the life and rise of Madeline Albright; I have found three particularly insightful: *Seasons of Her Life* by Ann Blackman, published by Scribner, 1998; *Madeline Albright and the New American Diplomacy* by Thomas Lippman, published by

Westview Press, 2000; and *Madeline Albright: A Twentieth-Century Odyssey* by Michael Dubbs, published by Henry Holt & Co., 1999.

17. For an interesting and thought-provoking handling of the subject of Renaissance friendship that will help further illuminate the issue and the thinking of Machiavelli and Castiglione on the subject, I recommend Dale Kent's *Friendship, Love and Trust in Renaissance Florence,* published by Harvard University Press, 2009.

18. For a demonstration of difficulties that attended Summers's abrasiveness and to see how his personality evolved over the years and his public image softened, I recommend you read *The Agenda: Inside the Clinton White House* by Bob Woodward, published by Simon & Schuster, 2005; *Confidence Men: Wall Street, Washington and the Education of a President* by Ron Suskind, published by Harper Publishing, 2011; "The Triumphalist," by John Cassidy for *The New Yorker,* July 6, 1998; "The Obama Memos," by Ryan Lizza for *The New Yorker,* January 30, 2012; and "Inside the Crisis," by Ryan Lizza for *The New Yorker,* October 12, 2009.

19. There are many sources that chronicle the battles between Jefferson and Hamilton. Among them, I refer you to *American Sphinx* by Joseph Ellis, published by Knopf, 1996; *Burr, Hamilton and Jefferson* by Roger Kennedy, published by Oxford University Press, 2000; *Alexander Hamilton* by Ron Chernow, published by Penguin Press, 2004; *Hamilton's Curse* by Thomas Dilorenzo, published by Crown Forum, 2008; *Jefferson v. Hamilton* by Noble Cunningham, published by St. Martin's Press, 2000; and *The Presidency of George*

Washington by Forrest McDonald, published by University of Kansas, 1974.

20. To say that during the second Bush administration Powell and Rumsfeld did not have a good working relationship would be an understatement. To see just how petty their battles could be as well as to understand the role that Armitage played in the process and for profiles of Colin Powell, Richard Armitage, and Donald Rumsfeld, see *The Survivor: Bill Clinton in the White House* by John Harris, published by Random House, 2006; *Soldier: The Life of Colin Powell* by Karen De-Young, published by Alfred A. Knopf, 2006; *State of Denial: Bush at War part III* by Bob Woodward, published by Simon & Schuster, 2006; *Plan of Attack: The Definitive Account of the Decision to Invade Iraq* by Bob Woodward, published by Simon & Schuster, 2004; and *Bush at War* by Bob Woodward, published by Simon & Schuster, 2002.

21. Cyrus Vance was at a disadvantage in his fight with Brzenzski for more reasons than just because he was the most gentlemanly of the two. President Carter did not trust the decision-making process at the State Department and wanted a national security structure that marginalized its influence. Because Vance permitted Brzenzski to design the process by which the president was advised on foreign affairs issues, Brzenzski was able to control the process. Brzenzski also had the advantage of being in the presence of the president more often than Vance. Brzenzski visited the Oval Office so frequently that the scheduler gave up keeping track. And Brzenzski ensured that his influence was never watered down by insisting that he be present at all meetings that

had a national security component—that often meant meetings where Vance was in attendance. The turf battles between Vance and Brzenzski can be viewed up close and personal in *An Outsider in the White House: Jimmy Carter, His Advisors and the Making of Foreign Policy* by Betty Glad, published by Cornell University Press, 2009; *Keeping the Faith: Memoirs of a President* by Jimmy Carter, published by University of Arkansas, 1995; *Working in the World: Jimmy Carter and the Making of Foreign Policy* by Robert A. Strong, published by Louisiana State University Press, 2000; and *Running the World: The Inside Story of the National Security Council and the Architects of American Power* by David Rothkopf, published by Public Affairs, 2006.

22. Lincoln did favor Seward and trusted him and often sought out his advice because their personalities meshed well. Chase was a good man, but he never really got over his loss of the nomination to Lincoln and resented him for it. Doris Kearns Goodwin writes a riveting account of how this incident unfolded in her masterwork *Team of Rivals: The Political Genius of Abraham Lincoln*, published by Simon & Schuster, 2006.

23. This vignette was adapted from the book *General of the Army* by Edward Gray, published by W. W. Norton & Co., 1990.

Made in the USA
Middletown, DE
16 January 2024

47969294R00135